Divine Therapeia and the Sermon

Divine Therapeia and the Sermon

Theocentric Therapeutic Preaching

Neil Pembroke

PICKWICK *Publications* · Eugene, Oregon

DIVINE THERAPEIA AND THE SERMON
Theocentric Therapeutic Preaching

Pickwick Publications
An Imprint of Wipf and Stock Publishers
199 W. 8th Ave., Suite 3
Eugene, OR 97401

www.wipfandstock.com

ISBN 13: 978-1-62032-440-0

Cataloguing-in-Publication data:

Pembroke, Neil.

    Divine therapeia and the sermon : theocentric therapeutic preaching / Neil Pembroke.

    xii + 147 pp. ; 23 cm. Includes bibliographical references.

    ISBN 13: 978-1-62032-440-0

    1. Pastoral counseling. 2. Preaching. 3. Christianity—Psychology. I. Title.

BV4012.2 P37 2013

Manufactured in the U.S.A.

Contents

Introduction

THERAPEUTIC PREACHING HAS ITS fair share of critics. The primary reason is that the term is often associated with a form of preaching in which the gospel is psychologized. Common forms of human suffering such as anxiety, depression, workplace stress, relationship problems, and grief and loss are addressed from the pulpit and mini-doses of therapy are administered to ease the pain. Preaching, rightly understood, is a liturgical announcement of the grace of God in Christ. What the therapeutic preachers give us instead, so the complaint goes, is half-baked serves of psychotherapy. I decided to write this book because I am convinced that though therapeutic preaching has been suffering from a malaise, it can be rehabilitated. What we need is *theocentric* therapeutic preaching. In my experience, this approach results in a rich conversation between grace and psychotherapy that is deeply healing.

I felt a little strange at first about including the word "theocentric" in the book's subtitle: *Theocentric Therapeutic Preaching*. After all, the essential theme of the Bible is God's providential and redemptive activity in the history of Israel and in the life, death, and resurrection of Christ. If the role of preaching is to name that activity in the contemporary context, how could it be anything else but theocentric? The problem with too much of what sits under the banner of therapeutic preaching is that the preacher loses sight of this crucially important truth. Human solutions get shifted to center stage. To be sure, God makes an appearance from time to time, but God's role is little more than a cameo. The first and all-important principle that needs to be established in responsible therapeutic preaching (and in any style of preaching for that matter) is theocentrism.

One wonders why some preachers shift God off to the wings. It probably has a great deal to do with what Henri Nouwen calls the problem of the "redundancy of the message": "Practically nobody listens to a sermon with the expectation of hearing something they did not already know. They have heard about Jesus—His disciples, His savings, His miracles, His death and resurrection . . . so often and in so many different ways and forms that the last thing they expect to come from the pulpit is any news."[1] With this in mind, one way that some preachers attempt to make the sermon newsworthy is to say little about the central characters in the biblical story that their listeners have heard so much about—God, Christ, and the Holy Spirit—and say a lot about the ideas of their favorite psychologists or psychotherapists. They think that delivering a newsworthy sermon requires sidestepping sin and grace and jumping on the psychological bandwagon.

In this book, I present a positive alternative. My proposal is that therapeutic preaching is rightly construed as pointing listeners to the divine *therapeia*. God's therapy is God's healing love expressed through compassion, acceptance, help, and forgiveness, but also through confrontation and challenge. God knows our human experience through and through. We are regularly assailed by stresses and strains; we need divine understanding, comfort, and help. But we are also regularly tempted to avoid the hard questions, the difficult choices, and the costly actions. We have a tendency to make regression choices that take us away from the way of Christ. God knows that we often need to hear the challenging word that calls us to progression choices.

There is a particular style of theocentric therapeutic preaching that I have in mind. I propose that counseling theory has an important role to play in preaching divine *therapeia*. There are those who may be quite happy with the suggestion that therapeutic preaching is essentially naming the divine *therapeia*, but who will eschew integration of counseling theory into the sermon. Here I am thinking especially of those who align themselves with the Barthian and postliberal positions. Their argument is that when a preacher comes to a text on God's *therapeia* with counseling theory in hand, it is inevitable that she will mold the message to fit the theory. That is, the message in the text is not allowed to unfold according to its natural shape; it is bent and twisted to fit the shape of the counseling theory. There is certainly considerable force to this argument. The temptation to make the text fit the psychological theory is indeed quite strong. Obviously, I am of the view that the temptation can be resisted. There is risk involved, but the pay-off associated with a correlational approach to therapeutic preaching makes the risk worthwhile. The psychological theory sheds its own unique

---

1. Nouwen, *Creative Ministry*, 25.

and penetrating light. It offers valuable insights and perspectives that are not otherwise available. In the end, it is a matter of judgment as to whether a particular piece of correlational work distorts or enlightens the message. Two sample sermons are offered in the final chapter. The reader will make her or his own assessment of the contribution—or lack thereof—that the correlational element makes to the particular sermon.

The particular from of correlational work that is advocated in the model involves the use of analogy. Counseling psychology can be gainfully employed to fund analogues that are not only illustrative of God's therapeutic action portrayed in the Scripture passage, but which also have the power to stimulate openness to that therapeutic action. That is to say, the analogical theology that takes place in the sermon is not simply didactic; it is also catalytic of increased receptivity to divine *therapeia*.

Roman Catholic and Protestant theologians have debated with each other for a very long time over the right understanding of analogical God-talk. Two main approaches have been proposed—namely, *analogia entis* (the analogy of being) and *analogia fidei* (the analogy of faith). The former is associated with Catholic theology, the latter with theologians of the Word such as Karl Barth and Eberhard Jüngel. In very general terms, the analogy of being assigns primacy to knowledge of the being of God, while the analogy of faith privileges knowledge of the action of God received through faith. While some Protestant theologians flatly reject the analogy of being, I contend that it is appropriate to incorporate it into theological reflection, as long as it is subordinated to the analogy of faith. I further contend that when we use therapeutic analogues in pastoral preaching, we need to take our lead from the analogy of faith, while at the same time incorporating the analogy of being. *Analogia fidei* in the context of a therapeutic sermon refers to a faithful proclamation of the divine *therapeia* through "qualified words"[2]—words that bear a likeness to the divine reality to which they point. The meaning of *analogia entis* in this setting is that reference to the way the loving being-with that is both the cornerstone of authentic therapy and part of the essential nature of human being is expressed gives us a revealing glimpse (it can only ever be a glimpse) of God's healing and acceptant love. In employing the analogy of being, a preacher needs to be careful lest she assign primacy in the analogical relation to human therapy. It should, of course, be assigned to God. God gives archetypal expression

---

2. On Barth's use of the term "qualified words," see McCormack, "Barth's Version of an 'Analogy of Being,'" 98–99.

to terms such as kindness, acceptance, and empathy; our expressions are ectypal. God's way of being loving, acceptant, and empathic represents a perfect realization of these virtues. Human expressions are defective reproductions of the perfect original.

Having presented the major proposals that will be developed in the book, it is necessary now to outline some of the other underlying principles and assumptions. The first point that I want to make probably goes without saying. It is this. In supporting the idea of therapeutic preaching, I do not mean to imply that I think that *all* preaching should be of this form. I do not even mean to give the impression that correlation with psychological insights should be a major emphasis in preaching. Divine *therapeia* should certainly be a central focus in preaching—remember that I take it to mean both God's comfort, help, and forgiveness on the one hand and God's challenge and confrontation on the other—but counseling theory should only be used when the text is particularly amenable to it.

A number of authors on preaching make the case for preaching as forming a community of faith and character.[3] It naturally follows that a major bone of contention for them in relation to therapeutic preaching is its individualistic focus. It is certainly true that the Bible tells the story of God calling first Israel and then the church into covenant relationship. The biblical picture is one of God at work forming a faithful people. As soon as one turns to psychotherapeutic psychology, however, the focus inevitably shifts to the individual. Therapy is mostly concerned with helping individuals experience healing, liberation, and growth. I agree that preaching is first and foremost concerned with forming a faithful and courageous Christ-centered community. That is why I do not think that the form of preaching that I discuss in this book should dominate the pulpit. It is not a therapeutic model of preaching that I am arguing for. Rather, what I am arguing for is *a model for good therapeutic preaching.*

The third principle for therapeutic preaching that I am advancing is that it needs to be construed quite broadly. It is not simply about helping hurting and confused individuals to cope. There is an element of (sensitive) confrontation in it also. Having said that, I do take on board Paul Scott Wilson's important point concerning the centrality of grace in the sermon.[4] Wilson argues that preaching can be so dominated by a

---

3. See, for example, Campbell, *Preaching Jesus*; Northcutt, *Kindling Desire*; and Ramsey, *Care-full Preaching.*

4. See Wilson, *The Four Pages.*

challenge to the faithful to be ever more zealous in witness, acts of mercy, and the advancement of justice and peace that parishioners come away from worship feeling heavy-laden and overwhelmed by responsibility. Preaching needs to celebrate God's grace and mercy. However, there is certainly a place for challenge. There is a coincidence between preaching and therapy here. The effective therapist is the one who knows when and how to appropriately confront a client. It is considerations such as these that lead me to view therapeutic preaching as offering both the comfort of God and the challenge of God.

The final principle is that while it is easy to insist that integration with counseling theory should not distort the essential message of the text, it is very difficult to achieve it in practice. Here I am reminded of a scene that is repeated a number of times in the classic Australian comedy, *The Castle*. Darryl Kerrigan is a loveable character with a good heart. He is a simple man who is completely lacking in style and sophistication. His wife regularly dishes him up very ordinary, well-known dishes, but he is quite overwhelmed by them and he thinks that they must be some new and exotic form of cuisine. I can't remember the scenes exactly, but they run something like this. Darryl says to his wife, Sal, "What do you call this, luv?" Sal looks at him quizzically, and after a short pause, replies, "Spaghetti Bolognaise." Darryl looks up and responds with, "Yeah, but it's the way you do it, luv." There is an art to the correlational work involved in preparing a good therapeutic sermon. The steps in the recipe are simple; but it's the way you do it that counts.

I have already indicated the main steps in the recipe for theocentric therapeutic preaching. Here is how they will be developed in the pages that follow. The first chapter consists of a critical survey of the major attempts in the twentieth century to correlate preaching and counseling. The overview and the analysis are used to develop a set of principles associated with responsible therapeutic preaching. In the second chapter, the model of therapeutic preaching that is proposed is outlined. The principles derived from the work in chapter 1 are incorporated, along with others that are developed in later chapters. The theme of chapter 3 is theocentric preaching. A number of important and influential approaches to locating God in Christ at the center of the sermon are surveyed. In the course of this survey, the issue of correlational preaching is raised. This crucial issue is pursued in much greater detail in chapter 4. As was indicated above, a particular form of correlational work is associated with the model of therapeutic preaching that I propose—namely, using counseling theory to fund metaphors for and analogues to divine *therapeia*. The issues around doing analogical theology in the preaching context are explored in chapter 5. In the final chapter, two sample sermons with commentary are presented.

Now that the reader has an overview of the work to be done, we will turn to the first task. That task is a critical survey of leading twentieth-century attempts to integrate preaching and counseling.

1

Preaching and Counseling in Dialogue

An Historical Overview

As I INDICATED IN the introduction, an important aspect of the model of therapeutic preaching that is proposed is the use of analogues to the divine *therapeia* drawn from counseling theory. In this chapter, a number of approaches to the relationship between preaching and counseling are surveyed in order to set the context for my own work. Moreover, critical engagement with the various approaches will serve to point up both positive practices and potential dangers.

Though there are clear similarities between preaching and counseling, the differences between the two are also very apparent. Perhaps the most obvious difference is that counseling involves a person-to-person dialogue, whereas in preaching it is almost always the case that only the person in the pulpit speaks. A second manifest difference is that counseling is directed to an individual or to a small group, whereas preaching involves communication to a large group—or at least large compared to the small groups that are associated with counseling. Then there is the fact that counseling works with psychological theory, while preaching is first and foremost a theological enterprise. A fourth difference has to do with the fact that counseling is (most often) construed as a nondirective process; it is the client who sets the agenda for the therapeutic work. In the preaching context, on the other hand, the agenda for the encounter is set by God's redeeming Word. There are no doubt other points of difference that could be listed. But enough has been said to indicate that scholars seeking to integrate the two endeavors need to get over some hurdles. Over the past eighty or so years, there have been a number of attempts to set up a fruitful dialogue between preaching and counseling. These approaches are critically analyzed below. They are grouped according to the following four categories: Preaching is counseling in a group setting (Harry Emerson Fosdick, Edgar N. Jackson, and Arthur L. Teikmanis); preaching and counseling operate according to the same basic process (David Switzer, Donald Capps, and Randall Nichols); preaching and counseling share a common theological base (Thomas Oden, Asa R. Sphar, and Argile Smith); and preaching and counseling can be integrated around a particular activity (Edward Wimberly [storytelling] and James Wallace [image production]). The chapter begins, however, with attention to a figure who exerted enormous influence on North American preaching in the twentieth century, and indeed continues to have an impact—namely, Harry Emerson Fosdick. In discussing Fosdick's "project method," attention will also be given to those in the therapeutic preaching movement who were inspired by him.

Preaching as Counseling for a Group

Harry Emerson Fosdick famously stated that "preaching can be personal consultation on a group scale."[1] This was an idea that gained considerable traction among American preachers in the twentieth century. In the fifties and sixties, when writers addressed the issue of preaching and pastoral care, it was this principle that usually guided their approach. For example, in his book *Preaching and Pastoral Care* Arthur Teikmanis states his conviction that "dynamic preaching is basically pastoral care in the context of worship."[2] In a similar vein, Edgar Jackson, in writing on preaching to people's needs, declares that the sermon can be used as "an instrument of group therapy."[3] Fosdick recalls that what planted the seed of this new approach to preaching was a counseling experience with a young man "from one of the church's finest families" who was in the grip of alcoholism. Fosdick tells the story this way:

> I recall my desperate feeling that if the gospel of Christ did not have in it available power to save that youth, of what use was it? When months of conference and inward struggle ended in triumph, when that young man said to me, "If you ever find anyone

1. Fosdick, "Personal Counseling," 12.
2. Teikmanis, *Preaching and Pastoral Care*, 19.
3. Jackson, *How to Preach*, 11.

who doesn't believe in God, send him to me—I know!" something happened to my preaching that courses in homiletics do not teach. *This* was the kind of effect that a *sermon* ought to have. It could deal with real problems, speak directly to individual needs, and because of it transforming consequences could happen to some person then and there.[4]

As we follow the outline of Fosdick's approach, we will see that the three aspects identified in the last sentence of the extract are absolutely central. For Fosdick, preaching the saving gospel of Christ is fundamentally about addressing *real* problems, aiming one's message at an individual need, and expecting that lives will be made-over as a result.

In an article published in *Harper's Magazine* in 1928 entitled, "What is the Matter with Preaching?"[5] Fosdick begins by pointing out what he sees as the deficiencies in both expository and topical preaching. In the expository form of proclamation that Fosdick was familiar with,[6] the preacher begins by elucidating a scriptural passage. Then she or he proceeds to a description of the historical setting. The next step in the process is to identify the meaning of the text for its own time and culture. The meaning of the text is then developed more fully by referring to the theology and moral stance of the author. This is followed by an attempt to communicate the application of the truth(s) contained in the passage. Finally, there is an exhortation to accept the truth offered and to put it into practice in daily living. According to Fosdick, though there is certainly value in expository preaching, the problem is that most often it is simply done poorly. The preacher gets lost in the historical setting and in the intricacies of the theology of the author. The result is bored, disinterested hearers: "Who seriously supposes that, as a matter of fact, one in a hundred of the congregation cares to start with, what Moses, Isaiah, Paul, or John meant in those special verses, or came to church deeply concerned about it?"[7] What makes a sermon a sermon rather than an exposition or a lecture is that it has for "its main business the head-on, constructive meeting of some problem which is puzzling minds, burdening consciences, distracting lives, and no sermon which so meets real human difficulty, with light to throw on it and power to win victory over it, can possibly be futile."[8]

4. Fosdick, "Personal Counseling," 12 (emphasis in the original).
5. Fosdick's article has been reprinted. See Fosdick, "What's the Matter?," 7–19.
6. See Fosdick, *The Living of These Days*, 52.
7. Fosdick, "What is the Matter?," 9.
8. Fosdick, "Personal Counseling," 12–13.

It might be assumed that Fosdick would be much kinder to the topical preachers. Not so. He chastises them for "turning their pulpits into platforms and their sermons into lectures, straining after some new, intriguing subject . . ."[9] In essence, the problem is that the topical preachers start "at the wrong end." They think first of their own ideas, when they should be thinking first of the people they will be preaching to. According to Fosdick, it is not a matter of coming up with a novel and intriguing topic to preach on but rather of focusing one's mind on the real needs of the people in the congregation.

Fosdick offers his "project method" as a superior approach. Edmund Linn offers the alternative designation, "the counseling sermon," for this innovative approach.[10] Even though the "counseling" is offered to a group, it is nevertheless "a conversational message from soul to soul."[11] Such preaching is not simply the presentation of helpful information; it should have the power to bring renewal and healing to suffering and confused persons. That is to say, the goal of the counseling sermon is the transformation of persons. "The preacher should go into his pulpit expecting that lives will be made over, families will be saved, young people will be directed into wholesome paths, potential suicides will become happy and useful members of society, and doubters will become vibrant believers."[12]

In presenting his project method, Fosdick draws a parallel with the innovative pedagogy of his time. The new teaching approach starts not with the subject but with the pupil. "Even the food which the child eats for breakfast, coming from the ends of the earth, is used to fascinate his interest in other lands; and we find our children getting at their mathematics by measuring the cubic space of the front parlor . . ."[13] What this says to preachers, according to Fosdick, is that they should concentrate their homiletic efforts on the concrete problems that the members of the congregation are struggling with.

In the project method, the preacher takes a cooperative approach. He or she is "not so much dogmatically thinking for [the listeners] as cooperatively thinking with them."[14] What this means is that the preacher needs to imaginatively project himself or herself into the inner world of his

9. Fosdick, "What is the Matter?," 11.

10. See Linn, *Preaching as Counseling*, 15.

11. Ibid.

12. Ibid., 16.

13. Fosdick, "What is the Matter?," 12.

14. Ibid.

or her listeners. Fosdick sees "clairvoyance" as an essential quality if preaching is to be transformative. The preacher needs to have a good sense of the objections, questions, and doubts residing in the minds of the listeners. In his biography of the great preacher, Robert Miller picks up on Fosdick's own talent for clairvoyance, observing that he "possessed an almost spooky seismographic sensitivity to what was troubling the minds and burdening the hearts of the citizens of the twentieth century."[15]

Fosdick uses the case of joy to illustrate his method.[16] The preacher should not start with joy in the fifth century, or with joy as a subject for a lecture, but with the concrete difficulties that people face as they attempt to live joyfully. This means that the preacher will cooperatively converse with his or her auditors on matters such as their mistaken ideas of joy, the reasons why joyful living is difficult for them to achieve, and the problem of victorious living in the face of the stresses and challenges of modern living. But the real sermon is not simply a conversation about joy; it goes further and actually produces it. "All powerful preaching is creative. It actually brings to pass in the lives of the congregation the thing it talks about."[17]

Fosdick's contention that preaching is fundamentally about using the gospel to meet the real needs of people in the congregation has exerted an enormous influence on preachers in North America and in many other countries throughout the world. When the sermon is focused on vitally important human concerns that have a clear connection to the central themes in the Scriptures—concerns such as shame and guilt, anxiety and despair, faith and hope, justice and peace, and the need for communion— this is laudable. Too often, however, the approach that is taken trivializes and degrades both the message of the gospel and the ministry of preaching. Preachers do no credit to themselves or to the Word they seek to minister when they direct their attention to matters such as time management, boosting self-esteem, and making the most of leisure time.[18]

The writers from the fifties and sixties drawn to therapeutic preaching established the meeting of individual needs as the major priority for the preacher. In setting the scene for his approach in *How to Preach to People's Needs* (1956), Edgar Jackson cites empirical research by Harold Rupp

---

15. Miller, *Harry Emerson Fosdick*, 374.

16. Fosdick, "What's the Matter?," 16–17.

17. Ibid., 16.

18. Cf. Long, "No News," 147.

involving a survey that received 4000 responses.[19] Approximately half of those surveyed indicated that they were troubled by issues such as futility, insecurity, loneliness, marriage problems, sex, alcoholism, false ideas of religion and morals, inferiority, and guilt. About a quarter of the cohort referred to concern over issues such as family problems, child training, infidelity, and separation and divorce. The remainder expressed concern over social, community, and national problems, along with "the more traditional religious concerns." Jackson avers that the pastor who wants to preach with "soul-healing power" needs to take cognizance of these needs and address them at both a psychological and a faith level. In his book, he covers virtually all of the personal issues raised in the survey responses, along with a number not mentioned. The structure he employs consists of addressing the issue psychologically, theologically, and homiletically, and then proceeding to provide sermon outlines which are accompanied by a brief commentary.

In order to get a feel for how Jackson goes about his work, two typical sermon outlines from his book are presented below. The first is entitled "Preaching to the Fearful," and the text is "God hath not given us the spirit of fear; but of power, and of love, and of a sound mind" (2 Tim 1:7).[20]

The first point made in the outline concerns the structure for the sermon. It is this: the "religious assurance" provided in the text suggests action on three levels. The first is the assurance of power. This is related to action on the physical level. The message is that when we are able to do something, our fear tends to subside.

The second level of action has to do with the healing power of the "spiritual resource of love." Many fear-producing situations are the result of a failure in love, goodwill, and understanding.

A "sound mind," lastly, is linked to an ability to think clearly. If we subject our fears to rational, clear-minded analysis, they usually dissipate.

In his commentary, Jackson observes that the "religious inspiration is implicit." God is the spiritual power behind the three resources available to us in combatting our fears.

The text for "Preaching to those bothered by alcohol," moving to the second typical example, is "O ye of little faith . . . Seek not ye what ye shall eat, or what ye shall drink, neither be ye of doubtful mind" (Luke 12:29).[21]

19. Jackson, *How to Preach*, 13–14.
20. Ibid., 43–44.
21. Ibid., 54–55.

It is suggested that Jesus is trying to help his listeners to gain a realistic perspective on life: "Persons of small faith seek after small things—food, drink, clothes—and in so doing they miss life's meaning. Those who put God first, on the other hand, find all that is needed to sustain life's important purposes."[22]

"Small faith" is established as the leitmotif of the sermon. Small faith is associated with an inadequate concept of God, of others, and of self. In commenting on this sermonic approach, Jackson observes that the problem of alcohol abuse is not tackled directly; rather, the underlying causes—false gods, small faith in people, and low self-esteem—are identified. The "antidote" is also offered—namely, an adequate concept of God and a true understanding of the creator–creature relationship.

We will get to critiques of Fosdick and the preaching-as-counseling school below, however it is worth noting in passing that Jackson falls into one of the common traps associated with this approach, viz., psychology rather than the redeeming action of God in Christ is given center stage. It is not that God and God's saving power are not mentioned. Rather, the problem is that God is seen largely as a spiritual resource that is available to us in our quest for personal wholeness and psychological integration. God is the power source that supports our quest for wholeness, joy, peace, and inner strength in the face of the high stresses and deep problems of modern living. The main focus is psychological self-help; God is identified as a spiritual power that supports self-help.

Arthur Teikmanis is similarly preoccupied with preaching to needs in *Preaching and Pastoral Care* (1964). However, his approach is broad in scope. As well as offering sermons on personal and interpersonal struggles, he takes up the issue of doctrines that may be causing consternation, along with pressing sociopolitical concerns. In relation to the first category, Teikmanis offers sermons addressing issues such as grief and loss, physical and mental illness, loss of self-esteem, relationship problems, anxiety, boredom, loneliness, and hostility. Amongst the central theological themes around which he considers that people are likely to experience doubt and uncertainty we find the following: God's Word and the Bible, miracles, prayer, and judgment. Finally, Teikmanis presents sermons on social and political issues such as Christian citizenship, the dangers of communism, racial and cultural crises, and poverty in America.

22. Ibid, 54.

What is striking, and quite concerning, about Teikmanis's work is that the sermons read more like public lectures than proclamations of the gospel. The text is simply a leaping-off point for the message that he wants to present. Upon reading a number of his sermons, a pattern begins to emerge. It is as follows. Teikmanis states at the beginning what the problem is. Then he explores the problem, making use of the insights of a number of experts in the field. One frequently find statements such as, "Dr. So and So [expert psychologist or sociologist] says . . ." or "The authors of *Spiritual Therapy* have discovered through their research that . . ." There is usually a brief reference to God's healing and strengthening power in the body of the sermon (and sometimes also in the introduction) along these lines: "If we but turn to God and seek God's grace . . ." and "We worry because we lack faith in God's care for us, in the truth that God supplies all our needs." The conclusion to the sermon recapitulates the message of God's healing and renewing grace: "God's grace is always sufficient; our pain and struggle is 'God's workshop' where character and spiritual maturity are forged." These theological references are always quite brief and are expressed in general terms. The affirmations of God's healing love and strengthening power are not taken from the text for the day; they are simply general affirmations that can be found in a number of places in the Scriptures. That is to say, we have here another demonstration of a major shortcoming in much therapeutic preaching: much more airplay is given to psychology than to the message of God's redeeming love in Christ.

Shifting the focus back to Harry Emerson Fosdick now, the first point to make is we are dealing here with one of the great preachers of the twentieth century. Nevertheless, there have been a number of criticisms leveled at his preaching-as-counseling approach. In the early sixties, Allan McDiarmid completed a doctoral thesis entitled, "A Critique of Harry Emerson Fosdick's Concept of Preaching as Counseling on a Group Scale."[23] McDiarmid's thesis is that preaching and counseling are discrete functions that cannot be combined. If McDiarmid means by this that preaching should not be construed as counseling, then he is correct. Preaching cannot be legitimately viewed as essentially an expression of another pastoral ministry, whether that ministry is pastoral counseling or something else. It would be just as unhelpful to claim that preaching is basically Christian education or evangelism or social action. Preaching is essentially a liturgical naming of God's redeeming love in Christ through the power of the Holy Spirit. What

---

23. Miller, *Harry Emerson Fosdick*, 346.

is being argued in this book, however, is that counseling theory provides a helpful set of images and analogues to convey (amenable parts of) the gospel in an engaging, newsworthy way. While it is right that a preacher should not attempt to counsel on a group scale, and it is also correct that proclamation should not normally feature in counseling, the two can be appropriately "combined" through setting up a mutually informing and renewing dialogue.

In response to Fosdick's contention that a preacher misses the mark unless he or she has insight into what is actually going on in people's lives, McDiarmid argues that Fosdick seems unaware that there is a body of truth that needs to be proclaimed regardless of the personal situation and needs of individuals.[24] It is certainly true that the gospel needs to be preached in its fullness; it is not legitimate to simply preach on a number of personal needs of parishioners that the pastor is sensitized to. Indeed, Fosdick was aware of this. He identifies the "most familiar and deplorable danger" associated with the project method as a limitation of the preacher's range. The preacher's "scope, like the Bible's, should include all human life, personal and social, and the whole message of the gospel."[25]

Another author of a doctoral thesis on Fosdick's approach to preaching, Harry Black Beverly, contends that his subject has forgotten that the central call upon the preacher is to proclaim the event of God's saving encounter with humankind in and through the life, death, and resurrection of Jesus Christ).[26] According to Beverly, Fosdick's message too often contained "no gospel to solve man's problems; no message about the redemptive acts of God in history on man's behalf; no witness to Christ as Lord and Savior . . ."[27] This loss of focus on God's redeeming work in Christ is perhaps the most common objection to Fosdick's method. Lee Ramsey in his critique of the Riverside preacher, for example, avers that "constant attention in preaching to the particular needs of the hearers, while admittedly retaining listener appeal, obscures the truth that God's answer to human suffering is already and ever again given in Christ."[28] Mike Graves laments the fact that too often preachers adopting a therapeutic approach fail to point their hearers to God's redeeming love. The focus is on human behavior; *we* get placed at the center of the preaching orbit. "We forget, grammatically

---

24. Ibid., 346.

25. Fosdick, "Personal Counseling," 14.

26. Miller, *Harry Emerson Fosdick*, 340–41.

27. Beverly, "Fosdick's *Predigtweise*," cited in Miller, *Harry Emerson Fosdick*, 340.

28. Ramsey, *Care-full Preaching*, 16.

speaking, that even if the *object* of our proclamation, what Fosdick referred to as the 'main business,' is to speak a relevant word to our listeners, God remains the *subject*."[29] To give one last example, Tom Long contends that for Fosdick the real interest and action in preaching is using the gospel to solve personal problems, when it is really about giving the news that because of what happened in the Christ event life can never be the same again.[30]

Another common objection to therapeutic preaching is that it shrinks the orb of pulpit proclamation to a narrow concern with personal psychological struggles. David Buttrick has this to say: "Many, if not most American pulpits, following Fosdick and fanned by the existentialist fifties, have tumbled into a narrow personalism. As a result, the God the pulpit announces is a God no larger than the reflection of our psychological needs, a God who has no concern for social justice."[31] While this is no doubt generally true of therapeutic preachers, it is wide of the mark in relation to Fosdick—as we have already seen. A survey of his published sermons reveals that along with covering a wide range of personal and interpersonal concerns, he preached on issues of race, poverty and hunger, and war. It is also worth recalling that another therapeutic preacher whose approach we discussed above, Arthur Teikmanis, also moves therapeutic preaching beyond personal psychology to social responsibility. Nevertheless, Buttrick's point is an important one. It is indeed the case that the preaching-as-counseling school is generally very prone to "narrow personalism." The position that I take is that while therapeutic preaching is an important form of preaching, it is only *one* form. The Scriptures address personal and interpersonal conflict and distress, but they also speak to social, political, economic, and environmental concerns. A pastor's preaching needs to have a wide scope.

Fosdick and others taking the preaching-as-counseling approach have also been criticized for taking their message to the text.[32] That is, the preacher uses her "clairvoyance" to discern an important "real need" that urgently requires pulpit attention and then searches for a text to attach it to. A read through a portion of sermons by Fosdick and others indicates that this indeed seems to be the case. The text for the day is often used as a springboard from which to leap into the real business of the address, be it anxiety, inferiority feelings, depression, dealing with pressure, or some

29. Graves, "God of Grace," 110 (emphasis in the original).

30. Long, "No News," 150.

31. Buttrick, "Preaching in an *Unbrave* New World," 12.

32. See, for example, Wilson, *Concise History of Preaching*, 160.

other psychological problem. Fosdick's biographer, Robert Miller, argues that this criticism is wide of the mark. Miller observes that in a number of his addresses and writings Fosdick states that the Bible is at the center of his preaching.[33] Miller goes on to offer his opinion that while others who used the project method virtually jettisoned the Scriptures in their fervor to touch the real needs of their listeners by drawing on the best of contemporary psychological, sociological, and philosophical wisdom, this was not the case with Fosdick himself. Fosdick, Miller contends, "sought to get at both the basic experiences of the Bible and those of his people and then he tried to bring the two together."[34] It is true that in his sermons Fosdick does seek to correlate ideas drawn from the Bible with those drawn from the psychological and philosophical thinking of his day in order to help his people in their personal and social struggles. For example, in his sermon entitled, "Winning the War of Nerves," he quotes the psychologist Dr. William Burnham: "The most drastic and usually the most effective remedy for fear is direct action."[35] He also observes that a perilous situation "splendidly aroused the powers" of the apostle Paul, and that he showed himself to be a man of action.[36] It may be true to say the Fosdick's preaching was Bible-centered to the extent that he mined the Bible for truths that speak to the needs of his people. It is not true, however, to say that it is Bible-centered preaching in the sense of allowing the text to speak on its own. It is only very rarely that Fosdick directs his attention in a sustained manner to teaching that can be drawn out of the text. When he does so, there is a sense that he is really grasped by the power of the biblical witness to speak light and life. In his sermon entitled "How to Stand Up and Take It," his text is a word from Ezekiel: "The Spirit entered into me, and set me upon my feet."[37] His point of departure is the observation that just as the world threw some deeply challenging and distressing situations at the prophet, so it is with us. Rather than simply taking an idea or two from Ezekiel's experience that supports what he wants to say via the psychological gurus about standing up under pressure, Fosdick stays with the prophet and wrestles truth and light out of his experiences:

33. Miller, *Harry Emerson Fosdick*, 348.

34. Ibid., 349.

35. Fosdick, *Living Under Tension*, 21.

36. Ibid., 26.

37. Ibid., 92–101.

- Ezekiel's experience is a parable for us. All around the prophet the exiled people are falling to pieces. But the Spirit entered into Ezekiel and gave him the power to stand up in the face of adversity.

- Ezekiel had to first tackle himself before tackling the situation. "That man had sessions with himself."[38]

- Ezekiel is just like us. He had times of self-pity, anxiety, depression, and resentment. But God was insistent: play the man and stand up and take it.

- A situation of adversity can call out the best in a person. The prophet saw that he could become a real man—not despite the exile, but because of it.

- Ezekiel approached the difficulties that he faced in such a way that they did not unmake him but rather made him.

- Great souls—Ezekiel, Moses, Jesus—have had their powers called out of them by the difficulties they have faced.

- Ezekiel was fitted by nature with "certain psychological powers" to be used in times of crisis (Fosdick concentrates on pugnacity).

- Ezekiel caught a fresh vision of God and his purposes for Israel. Ezekiel "belonged to something greater than himself."[39] He thought not of himself but of Israel and God's purposes for it. Ezekiel "believed in the unbelievable."

- Fosdick indicates that he is not suggesting that we can tackle difficulty and overcome it through our own unaided efforts. The Spirit *entered into* Ezekiel. The prophet did not set himself on his feet; he was set on his feet. This is the heart of religion: opening oneself to the power of Almighty God.

Though, as this example clearly indicates, Fosdick does sometimes engage the text quite fully, most often it is simply a prime for his homiletic pump. It gets his creative juice flowing as he begins his exploration of what presents as a pressing issue for his people. To be sure, the text finds its way into the body of the sermon and is used a number of times to reinforce, highlight, or expand this or that teaching point. But it is the issue rather than the text that is the center of gravity in most of Fosdick's sermons.

38. Ibid., 94.
39. Ibid., 100.

One final criticism comes from Kay Northcutt. She contends that Fosdick and contemporary adherents of the preaching-as-counseling approach view suffering as something to be avoided, when it is actually something to be entered into as an inevitable dimension of the Christian way of life.[40] Experiences of suffering such as loneliness, anxiety, temptation, and the experience of limit are "necessary to the full experience and joy of being human."[41] While I take Northcutt's point that human existence has suffering built into it, a nuancing of her objection would have been helpful. There are indeed some forms of suffering that are a normal and unavoidable part of human existence. This type of distress I would call *existential suffering.* Human beings cannot avoid being lonely, feeling anxious, being assailed by "the blues" occasionally, suffering loss and grief, falling ill, tasting the bitter pill of failure, to mention just some of the painful experiences that are part and parcel of human existence. There is another type of distress, however, namely *pathological suffering.* This type of suffering is *not* normal for human beings. Some of us torture ourselves unnecessarily. It is possible to gain significant relief from pathological grief, neurotic guilt, toxic shame, and other self-defeating attitudes and behaviors. Counseling and psychotherapy are the main avenues for help here, but therapeutic preaching can also make an important contribution.

The reason for highlighting this distinction between existential and pathological suffering is to register the objection that making bald statements such as "suffering is necessary to the full experience and joy of being human" is not helpful. It works well when we are talking about certain universal human experiences such as loneliness, temptation, illness, and grief; it is unhelpful in the context of pathological mental suffering. We do not want to give people gripped by pathological suffering the message that their distress is a normal part of being human—something to be entered into as part of the fullness of the human experience. Now I do not think for a moment that Northcutt takes the view that pathological suffering is something to be simply endured in the name of growing into Christian maturity. However, the discussion above suggests that her criticism of therapeutic preachers in their approach to suffering needs to be more nuanced.

Despite the fact that there are clearly a number of deficiencies in the project method, a number of the underlying principles present as sound. First, the gospel *does* speak to real human needs. At its best, the method

40. Northcutt, *Kindling Desire*, 55.

41. Ibid.

advocates addressing not just concerns that are usually associated with counseling, but also ones that are overtly theological such as sin, doubt, faith, hope, and love, along with issues of social responsibility and action for peace and justice. The second principle in the method that is helpful is that good preaching is transformative. The transformation is not instantaneous—or at least not usually so. The normal pattern is that it takes time for God to work in a person through the agency of the preached Word. But when the talent, diligence, and faithfulness of the preacher joins with the Holy Spirit, on the one hand, and openness in the listener, on the other, preaching can bring a renewal of mind and soul that takes a person into a deeper experience of the peace and joy of Christ, and of worship, witness, and service. Finally, the strategy of achieving a correlation between the biblical approach to human experience and that of relevant voices from the contemporary culture (e.g., the psychologists, sociologists, and the philosophers) is a useful one (we will discuss this issue much more fully in chapter 4). At least it is useful when the text is allowed to speak for itself, rather than being twisted to fit a predetermined message crafted from the culture's best wisdom. Creative cultural self-interpretations need to be used in service of unfolding a message from the text—not the other way round.

We now move to a discussion on the work of three pastoral theologians who have observed that preaching and counseling exhibit a similar structure. The approaches of David Switzer, Donald Capps, and Randall Nichols differ at the level of detail, but what unites them is the underlying conviction that preaching and counseling theory can be profitably integrated.

Preaching and Counseling Have a Similar Structure

Though Switzer, Capps, and Nichols seek to identify points of strong similarity between the structures of the two activities, they do not wish to claim that preaching is counseling. Rather, they suggest that attending to the steps in the counseling process informs, illumines, and offers new possibilities for the craft of preaching.

Switzer, first, begins his discussion in *Pastor, Preacher, Person* (1979) by reflecting on the meeting of human need through preaching—a concern that is right at the heart of Fosdick's project method. He avers that "the gospel, no matter which aspect of it is being explicated, always speaks to some real and legitimate human need."[42] Switzer makes it clear, though, that he

---

42. Switzer, *Pastor, Preacher, Person*, 51.

is not saying that every sermon must address one or more of the issues and crises that typically arise in pastoral care and counseling: "Preaching in such a way as to meet person's [sic] needs does not imply that the pulpit is to be the regular weekly source of psychological self-help."[43]

Switzer rejects Arthur Teikmanis's statement that "dynamic preaching is basically pastoral care in the context of worship."[44] Preaching cannot be reduced to an act of pastoral care. Proclamation of the gospel is the attempt to use human words to point others to Jesus as the Word of God. The ministry of the Word, Switzer observes, is much broader than pastoral care. Nevertheless, preaching and pastoral counseling do exhibit some strong similarities. They are alike in that "they are both interpersonal, primarily verbal processes engaged in by the minister with others, and as such there are *some* common goals and necessary relational ingredients if they are to be facilitative."[45]

Switzer goes on to develop the connection between the two by showing that they share in the same basic structure or process.[46] The counseling process he outlines is as follows: Self-exploration → the setting of goals → evaluation of behavioral alternatives → decision-making → action. He observes that preaching is similar in that without the last two stages of decision-making and action on the part of the hearers there has been no sermon. While insight and inspiration are valuable in and of themselves, effective preaching takes an auditor further; it leads her into making a decision and acting upon it. (The reader will recall that a similar point is made by Fosdick. A sermon must produce the psychological strength, theological virtue, or course of action that it speaks to). Finally, to get to the point of action, most listeners will need to first engage in self-exploration and goal-setting. This integration by Switzer is all right as far as it goes, but in moving to the other two approaches, we will encounter correlative work that is both more sustained and more insightful.

In his book entitled, *Pastoral Counseling and Preaching: The Quest for an Integrated Ministry* (1980), Donald Capps takes a similar approach to Switzer—at least in general terms. The structure that he uses to integrate the two ministries, as is the case with Switzer, is drawn from counseling—though it is differently conceived. Capps' structure has four phases:

---

43. Ibid.

44. See ibid, 51. The quote comes from Teikmanis, *Preaching and Pastoral Care*, 19.

45. Switzer, *Pastor, Preacher, Person*, 53.

46. Ibid., 64–67.

(i) identification of the problem, (ii) reconstruction of the problem, (iii) diagnostic interpretation, and (iv) pastoral intervention.[47]

Capps suggests that diagnostic interpretation is the primary basis for the integration of pastoral counseling and preaching.[48] The majority of his book is devoted to this topic. Diagnosis is construed by Capps, following Paul Pruyser, as "making accurate discriminations in order to do the right thing . . ."[49] Capps suggests that this is an essential task in pastoral ministry. He further suggests that emphasis on the relationship between the counselor and the counselee in the diagnostic process has particular relevance for the integration of the two ministries. If it is the case that empathic relating in counseling leads to a more discriminating diagnostic process, this principle can be helpfully transferred to the preaching context.[50] That is to say, the preacher should abstain from an "external diagnostic attitude" and instead enter into the internal frame of reference of her listeners. (This is, of course, the point that Fosdick makes so insistently when he talks about the need for "clairvoyance.")

Another important point of integration has to do with resources for learning the art of theological diagnostics. According to Capps, the best source of guidance for doing theological diagnosis in counseling is the pastor's own use of theological diagnosis in her preaching each Sunday.[51] Another very valuable practice that he identifies is reading and analyzing published sermons.

In chapter 4, Capps identifies six types of theological diagnosis in sermons, and then proceeds to show how these can be effectively utilized in pastoral counseling. In presenting the six types, he suggests that homiletical diagnosis operates by (i) identifying underlying personal motivations, (ii) pointing up the range of potential causes of the problem, (iii) exposing inadequate formulations of the problem, (iv) drawing attention to untapped personal and spiritual resources, (v) bringing clarity to the problem, and (vi) assessing problems in terms of the deepest intentions of shared human experience. He argues that most, if not all, of these types are already explicitly used in pastoral counseling. However, the associated theological dynamics are not always made explicit. Capps' approach is to

47. Capps, *Pastoral Counseling and Preaching*, 36–37.

48. Ibid., 62.

49. Ibid., 76.

50. Ibid., 77.

51. Ibid., 89.

discuss how these diagnostic types are used psychologically and then to use approaches in sermons by famous preachers to point up the matching theological principles.[52] The six theological principles that are connected to the six diagnostic types are these: (i) the will of God for one's life, (ii) God's encouragement of human responsibility and initiative, (iii) the experience of the grace of God, (iv) the constructive role of hope in God, (v) the central place for truth in our relationship to God, and (vi) communal dimensions of our relationship to God, especially in the form of active love.[53]

It is evident that Capps appreciates the need to give adequate attention to the Bible and theology in the quest for an integrated ministry. He is keenly aware that the therapeutic paradigm has tended to dominate pastoral theology. Even though he uses a therapeutic structure as the basis for the integration, and, moreover, employs a therapeutic action—diagnosis—to shape the whole discussion, in the end his work is thoroughly theological. It is the notion of *theological* diagnosis that he develops: the grace of God, hope in God, and God's call to responsible living are the central themes.

The final "structuralist" whose work we will discuss is Randall Nichols. A key term for Nichols in pointing up the connections between preaching and counseling is *pastoral communication*. He defines it as "that aspect of human communication which affects and involves the deeply personal in us and, moreover, which does so to some extent by the design and intention of the communicator."[54] Nichols indicates at the beginning of his book, *The Restoring Word* (1987), that he is not attempting to integrate preaching and pastoral care in the sense of trying to meld together two different pastoral ministries. Rather, he tells us that he intends to focus on the communicative linkage and the pastoral/therapeutic dimension of it. In doing this, Nichols builds the argument that the communicative structures in therapeutic work and pastoral preaching are very similar.

In developing his approach to what he sees as the "direct parallels" in the communicative structures of proclamation and counseling, Nichols indicates that he rejects Fosdick's notion that preaching is counseling on a group scale.[55] He begins his integrative work by asking the question, "What does a therapist do?" He suggests that, in essence, a therapist, (a) gives

---

52. Ibid., 108ff.

53. Ibid., 115.

54. Nicholls, *The Restoring Word*, 13.

55. Ibid., 67.

permission for certain things, (b) reframes issues, and (c) teaches good communication.[56] Pastoral preaching does these same things.

A therapist, first, gives permission to the client to feel things she is afraid of feeling or thinks she is not allowed to feel, to experience what is going on for her more fully and consciously, and to look at things from different, perhaps taboo, perspectives. From a theological viewpoint, Nichols observes, this permission-giving is a form of blessing.

Reframing, second, is a stock tool of the trade for therapists. The image that it is based on is the way in which a painting looks quite different when its frame is changed. In the same way, the client's situation will appear very different when it is set in a new frame. The therapist facilitates a process of reformulating the problem and how it is viewed. For example, a perfectionistic mother suffering from deep feelings of shame, guilt, and inferiority over her perception of herself as "a bad mother," might be helped to see herself as a good mother who sometimes makes mistakes. Nichols sees a theological connection with prophesying. The prophet talks about current events in a very different way to the conventional approach. Put differently, he reframes the situation of the nation. His fellow Israelites consider that their behavior is perfectly acceptable and that their future will be one of peace and prosperity. Into this complacent setting marches the prophet with his strange proclamation that unless the people repent God will execute an act of judgment upon them. Their peaceful, happy life is about to be violently disrupted by an invading power or by some other catastrophic event.

Therapists, finally, teach their clients how to communicate effectively. In place of blaming, aggressive (or passive-aggressive), and defensive communication, they learn an honest, open, and empathic way of relating. The theological link for Nichols is *didache*. The Church teaches "communicative qualities of directness, interpersonal empathy, freedom from judgment, personal openness, honest expression of difficulties . . ."[57]

Nichols goes on to discuss five more elements in the structure of the therapeutic environment that parallel what goes on in pastoral preaching—namely, its "moratorium" quality, the way it gives responsibility, loaning a stronger sense of reality, the holding experience, and transference and modelling.[58] Therapy, first, creates a sanctuary experience. The client is afforded

---

56. Ibid., 67.

57. Ibid., 71.

58. I have taken the liberty of adding some descriptive material to that of Nichols's

the freedom to deal with all kinds of feelings, past history, impulses, conflicts, and desires secure in the knowledge that in this therapeutic space they are talked about, but no tension-filled action is required. During this moratorium, the client receives the healing, self-awareness, and inner strength to go out into the world beyond the therapist's office and to deal more realistically with the challenges of living. Nichols suggests that the same can be said of pulpit ministry: "Pastoral preaching presides over a 'sanctuary' experience *in service to* (never as a substitute for) the exile's return to a broken Jerusalem in need of rebuilding."[59]

The second element is the giving of responsibility. There is reluctance on the part of clients—and of many people who never feel a need for therapy, one might add—to take responsibility for what is going wrong in their lives. Projection of the problem onto others is very common. The therapist helps the client take responsibility for the issues in the counseling encounter so that she can gradually learn to take responsibility for them in the real world in which she lives. Similarly, pastoral preaching seeks to help people to live realistically and responsibly in the world. A central purpose of preaching, according to Nichols, is to assist people in their quest to deal directly and honestly with life as it is, using the guidance and resources of the Christian faith.[60]

Loaning a stronger sense of reality, moving to the third element, relates to an advantage that the therapist's background affords her. Through her own therapy and training, she is "relatively better able than others to deal with reality with a minimum of protective screens and buffers."[61] Nichols states that the term *loaning* is used to indicate the fact that "in the therapeutic relationship some of my sense of reality becomes available to my clients through a sort of confidence or guiding process . . ."[62] The connection with preaching is that the preacher offers to her listeners the resources of the Bible—faith, hope, and love—so that they may be able to look life, and death, in the face without being crushed or overwhelmed.

The idea of a holding environment—the fourth element—comes from the British pediatrician and psychiatrist, Donald Winnicott. Winnicott observes that a fundamental developmental step for a young child involves

in an attempt to bring extra clarity to some of the therapeutic concepts he works with.

59. Nichols, *The Restoring Word*, 30 (emphasis in the original).

60. Ibid., 30.

61. Ibid., 77.

62. Ibid., 78.

moving from the experience of merger with the environment to one in which she is able to distinguish between herself and others. He identifies three spheres in human psychological experience: the subjective, the objective, and the intermediate or transitional. It is in the intermediate zone that the transition from the "oceanic feeling" (Freud) to "me and you" takes place. The child's mother creates a "holding" environment in which he is supported in this natural but very demanding transition. Nichols draws a parallel with the therapeutic encounter. The therapist creates a holding environment that allows people to make the transition from defending against reality to facing it honestly and openly. He then makes the link with proclamation: "[When I preach], I am holding people through their concerns and issues . . ."[63]

The final structural element that Nichols discusses is transference and modeling. The idea of transference comes from Sigmund Freud. Freud observed that many of his patients related to him as if he were another person—someone who was significant in their past. The anger, fear, and conflict associated with the relationship the patient shared with this third party were transferred to the present dialogue with Freud. Freud realized that the transference is actually a requirement for effective treatment. In the transference experience, the unconscious conflict is brought into the open and is therefore able to be processed. Nichols observes that in the transference, the therapist seeks to model a more healthy and whole interaction than was experienced with the particular person from the client's past. He finds a "strong parallel" with pastoral preaching. However, he is quick to point out that he is not suggesting that people see in the preacher an array of figures from their past (parents, teachers, lovers, etc.). Rather, "by dint of his or her traditionally vested authority in the pulpit . . . the preacher becomes a more-than-usually-significant figure for people when highly invested matters are talked about."[64]

That brings our discussion of the approaches of the structuralists to a close. It is interesting to note that the movement in drawing parallels between therapeutic and homiletic structures in all three cases is from counseling to preaching. Each pastoral theologian begins with the fundamental elements in counseling work and then points up the strong similarities with pulpit ministry. It might be suggested that since counseling has a relatively clear structure, it is logical to start with this. But preaching also has a readily

63. Ibid., 82.
64. Ibid., 85.

identifiable shape—though, as with counseling, this is given a different articulation by various homileticians. Preaching, for example, follows a movement from opening disequilibrium, through complication and decisive turn, toward resolution (the narrative structure of Eugene Lowry). Or preaching moves from trouble in the text to trouble in the world, and from grace in the text to grace in the world (the theological structure of Paul Scott Wilson). There seems to be no compelling reason for basing the integrative work in a counseling structure. Be that as it may, the important point is that the work of these three pastoral theologians, when taken as a whole, provides a comprehensive picture of the similarities between pulpit ministry and counseling. The next approach to be surveyed holds that counseling and preaching share a common theological foundation. We will discuss the work of Tom Oden, on the one hand, and of Asa Sphar and Argile Smith, on the other.

Preaching and Counseling Share a Common Theological Base

Tom Oden argues in *Kerygma and Counseling* (1966) the central thesis that *"there is an implicit assumption hidden in all effective psychotherapy which is made explicit in the Christian proclamation."*[65] This tacit assumption relates to a fundamental condition of therapy—namely, acceptance. It is not simply the case, Oden observes, that the therapist accepts the client; it is also the case that the client is considered acceptable as a human being by the ground of being itself.[66] In other words, the ultimate ground of all therapeutic work is the gracious and restorative love of God. Oden is "less concerned to say that God is like the therapist than that the therapist (perhaps even unwittingly) shares in the reality of God's healing in the midst of his work, and thus embodies that healing power."[67] That is to say, the God that is proclaimed from the pulpit—the God of all comfort, the source of all mercies, the fount of never-ending compassion, is the ontological stage on which the drama that is counseling is played out. The preacher explicitly deals with the theological truth that is implicit in counseling. The subject and object of the church's proclamation is God the *therapōn*.[68] The *therapeia* that he renders is redemptive love manifested in Jesus' ministry of healing the sick, casting out evil spirits, and forgiving sin. Thus, the New

65. Oden, *Kerygma and Counseling*, 9 (emphasis in the original).

66. Ibid., 21.

67. Ibid., 73.

68. Ibid., 150.

Testament presents Jesus as "the prototypical image of the *therapōn*."[69] He is the personification and the event of God's own intimate healing, redeeming service to humanity.

Oden contends that it is possible to correlate the divine activity (revelation), the therapist's actions (clarification), and the individual's response (growth toward authenticity). He makes the links in this way:[70]

God's Activity	Therapist's Actions	Individual's Response
Incarnation	Empathic understanding	Increased self-understanding
Divine congruence	Therapeutic congruence	Increased self-identity
Forgiveness	Acceptance	Increased self-acceptance
Grace	Permissiveness	Increased self-direction
Divine love	Unconditional positive regard	Increased love of others

These are all very plausible and helpful connections. Oden uses a particular method in undertaking this integrative work. Following Barth's *analogia fidei*, he moves from the Christ event to human experience. Oden's central claim is that the restorative work of the therapist is a reflection of and participation in God's definitive act of healing in and through the person and work of Christ.[71]

The theological motif that Asa Sphar and Argile Smith use in their book *Helping Hurting People* (2002)—moving to the second approach—to correlate proclamation and counseling is one that lies right at the center of the gospel, viz., reconciliation.[72] In developing their reconciliation-focused counseling (RFC) model, Sphar and Smith make the claim that alienation from God, others, and self is at the root of most, if not all, intrapsychic and interpersonal distress. There are, then, three fundamental relational zones in play here: the relationship with God, with others, and with self. The authors contend that the central task of the Christian counselor is to facilitate a process of restoration in these three relational areas: "We seek to set the stage for a divine-human encounter, in the midst of human tragedy and brokenness, in which grace is communicated and reconciliation is

---

69. Ibid.

70. Ibid., 49.

71. It will be evident to the reader that I use some of Tom Oden's terms and ideas in my own work. I am very indebted to him for his helpful and insightful analysis.

72. See Sphar and Smith, *Helping Hurting People*.

experienced in each relational domain."[73] The counselor is construed as a positive relational model.[74] That is, the counselor is "technique," by virtue of the fact that she brings personal strengths in the area of relationality that encourage the client in his cultivation of new relationships or enhancement of existing ones.

Sphar and Smith incorporate a number of psychotherapeutic approaches into their three stage model. Included are problem-solving, interpersonal, solution-focused, and cognitive-behavioral methods. The three stages are these: identifying the problem(s) (areas of alienation), the goals (targets of reconciliation), and the strategies (movement toward restoration/reconciliation).[75] Though the model as it unfolds looks quite similar to a number of counseling methods—in particular, those that take a brief therapy or solution-oriented approach—what sets it apart is that in each phase emphasis on reconciliation is incorporated.

The authors suggest that if a pastor reflects on RFC in the context of preaching, she will observe that the two ministries share a good deal of common ground. Both RFC and preaching have as their core concern helping alienated people restore broken relationships with God, others, and self through the grace of Christ's redemptive act.[76] This move of establishing both counseling and preaching on the theological foundation of reconciliation is a very strong one. Unfortunately, the way in which the authors develop their approach to pastoral preaching sometimes lacks depth and insight. I will indicate why I think this is the case below.

Sphar and Smith work with "biographical-narrative" Scripture passages in which the troubled experiences of the main character(s) are used to develop teaching points aimed at helping listeners deal with a similar issue.[77] One such biographical-narrative centers on Elijah's experience of sorrow and despair in the wake of Queen Jezebel's declaration that she would kill him (1 Kgs 19:1–18).[78] The address is entitled, "A Sermon about Depression: Getting Back on Track." The approach consists of retelling the story and then asking the listeners to identify with Elijah's experience—or at least with some aspects of it. Three teaching points are developed to assist those listeners who are struggling with depression: "After He refreshes us

73. Ibid., 26.

74. Ibid., 43.

75. Ibid., 86.

76. Ibid., 167.

77. Ibid., 168.

78. Ibid., 169–74.

with nourishment, rest [point 1], and a new sense of His presence [point 2], He wants us to get on with the work He intended us to do all along [point 3]."[79] The climax of the sermon consists of an assurance that in fighting our way out of depression we are not alone; we can rely on God's loving presence to strengthen us.

At the risk of sounding harsh, the approach taken in this sermon presents as bordering on simplistic. A listener suffering from depression could be forgiven for thinking that what she has been offered is little more than platitudes. Making sure that one takes adequate nourishment and gets good rest is certainly good advice. While looking after food intake is certainly quite manageable, dealing with insomnia is clearly not a simple matter for many depressed persons. Similarly, when in any kind of distress listening for the voice of God and trusting in God's loving presence are certainly very important practices for the Christian. But wouldn't any Christian—other than perhaps a very new one—be aware of this already? Tom Long writes of the importance of making sermons "newsworthy."[80] He observes that sermons too often consist of little more than reiteration of biblical truths that have been aired a thousand times. Sadly, there isn't much news in this sermon.

Other sermons provided by the authors also suffer from a failure to provide depth and insight. In the sermon entitled, "A Sermon about Confusion and Worry,"[81] the text is Luke 11:5–13. In this passage, Jesus teaches the disciples to pray, and assures them that if they ask they will receive. The main teaching point in the sermon is set out below:

> When God doesn't answer our prayer, we get confused and frustrated. In turn, the gap between us and God grows wider. Factor in the troublesome, haunting notion that God might be absent and the situation can get completely overwhelming. It can get to the point that [sic] may decide to give up on prayer altogether. Jesus diminishes the distance created by God's silence by assuring us that, indeed, God hears us. He encourages us to keep on asking, seeking, and knocking. At the right time, God will answer.[82]

This is certainly a good summary of an important spiritual truth. But might not a person beset by confusion and worry rightfully expect more from the preacher in the way of help than simply a restatement of what she

79. Ibid., 173.

80. See Long "No News."

81. Sphar and Smith, *Helping Hurting People*, 174–79.

82. Ibid., 178.

has already heard in the Bible reading? In sum, Sphar and Smith's strategy of integrating preaching and counseling around the theme of reconciliation is a good one; the practical application in the preaching area could be quite a bit stronger.

The last of our four approaches to the dialogue between preaching and counseling is concerned with shared practice. The two practices that we will look at are storytelling and image generation. The two pastoral theologians that feature here are Edward Wimberly and James Wallace, respectively.

Storytelling and Image Production As Link Terms

Edward Wimberly's aim in *Moving from Same to Self-Worth* (1994)[83] is to show how positive stories can be used in both pastoral counseling and preaching to help boost self-esteem in those plagued by shame feelings. Wimberly's method is to study the life of Jesus and draw implications for contemporary persons. He contends that though Jesus was consistently exposed to potentially shaming-inducing forces, he was not shame-prone.[84] Wimberly further contends that Jesus' sense of self-worth was significantly tied to his sense of mission and purpose. There is a lesson here for us, he suggests.

Wimberly observes that while storytelling has not usually been associated with pastoral counseling, in recent times a number of psychotherapists have begun to explore its use. The stories help people learn from the experience of Jesus as they seek to address a lack of meaning and purpose in their lives. Storytelling is construed as a "hermeneutical approach that assists in the meaning-making process."[85]

Wimberly's first move is to identify authentic sayings of Jesus. He then presents both a retelling of the biblical story and a contemporary narrative that closely parallels it. Wimberly suggests that he is making use of the power that is in story and parable to undermine the power in a person's present, unhealthy view of reality by offering a more positive, life-affirming view. He suggests that the parabolic approach is quite close to that of the "metaphoric protocol" that is used in some approaches to psychotherapy.[86] It is here that he establishes the link between pastoral counseling and preaching: "Building on these two distinct traditions of parable and

83. Wimberly, *Moving from Shame*.
84. Ibid., 39.
85. Ibid., 16.
86. Ibid., 15.

metaphor, I suggest that there is a convergence of pastoral counseling and preaching. This convergence recognizes that reality and the ways of knowing reality are storied, and changing one's view of reality requires attending to people's stories. Moreover, preaching and pastoral counseling are arenas where stories are told that change people's view of reality."[87]

This approach of identifying the power of story in both counseling and preaching is an excellent one. There is both ample psychological evidence and strong philosophical and theological argumentation available that lends support to the notion that human existence is a storied one; we structure our lives and construct our identities through narrative. Wimberly is tapping into an activity that is right at the heart of human experience. Moreover, as he observes, Jesus' parabolic ministry demonstrates very clearly the power of story to undermine faulty, unhealthy perceptions of reality and to offer hopeful, life-affirming ones.

Wimberly is opposed to a compartmentalizing of the two ministries. It is his contention that pastoral counseling alone cannot help a person replace the current shame-inducing story with one that sponsors self-love and feelings of worth. He makes a plea for a holistic approach that incorporates counseling, preaching, and participation in *koinonia*.[88] While I certainly appreciate the value in a total approach such as the one proposed by Wimberly, he may be guilty of overstating the case. There are surely many people who have been helped to move toward self-worth by both secular and pastoral counselors without the benefit of preaching and Christian fellowship. It is perhaps better to formulate the point in this way: A holistic approach involving pastoral counseling, the preached Word, and participation in a Christian community is the ideal for the disciple seeking to overcome shame-proneness; however, it is the case that some people are significantly helped by counseling or preaching interventions alone.

The category of story also features in James Wallace's approach; however, it is the use of images that he pays particular attention to in his book, *Imaginal Preaching* (1995). Wallace suggests that story can be thought of as an "extended imaginal experience."[89] It is often the case that a story is the bearer of a particular image. He tells the reader that in his own experience of preaching he has found that what really engages listeners is "such imaginal realities as metaphor and story."[90]

---

87. Ibid., 15–16.

88. Ibid., 18.

89. Wallace, *Imaginal Preaching*, 16.

90. Ibid., 3.

Wallace appreciates very much the work of James Hillman in *Insearch: Psychology and Religion*. He recognizes that the importance Hillman attaches to "soul-work" has implications for preaching.[91] The psychotherapist has shown him the importance of care for the soul that is grounded in "a psycho-spiritual appreciation for the cultivation of the imagination."[92]

In reflecting on the use of images in preaching, Wallace makes similar points to Wimberly—with a little help from some theological friends.[93] The first is that to be converted to Christ requires changing the images we have of God, self, and world (Elizabeth Achtemeier). The second one is that when preachers use images and story, they help their listeners "climb the ladder" up to truth (Tom Troeger). The third and final point is that the preacher's craft involves imagining a new reality—the reign of God—that subverts the conventional one (Walter Brueggemann). Wallace suggests that in order to utilize the power suggested in these perspectives, the "imaginal" preacher looks not for the key thought or concept in the story but rather for the primary image.

Wallace observes that images do important work. "They work for us, against us, in us, through us. They can transform us in our depths, move us toward the highest truth, motivate us to change the world, and ultimately influence the final outcome when we stand face to face with God."[94] Wallace is very impressed with the philosopher Rubem Alves' insight that images have the power to possess those who see them. But in the context of preaching, shouldn't we be emphasizing the theological dimension of the transformative experience? Wallace recognizes this dimension when he surveys the work of his chosen theologians, but in this summary of the power of image in preaching, it is nowhere to be seen. Images are powerful in preaching, I contend, because God inspires their use in the preparation of the sermon and then conveys them through the preacher to the hearts, minds, and souls of her listeners. Those of us who preach, sometimes lose heart because we sense that our potentially powerful, life-changing, and renewing gospel images seem to be missing the mark. To this somewhat depressing situation Fred Craddock puts this question: "Why, then, preach, if words ricochet off deaf ears and fall unheard to the sanctuary floor?" His answer is thoroughly theological: "Because God opens ears, because God's prevenient grace makes the heart capable of hearing the gospel, because

91. Ibid.
92. Ibid.
93. Ibid., 17.
94. Ibid., 18.

the same Spirit that inspires the Word works to make the listener receptive. With the Holy Spirit operative at both mouth and ear, all praise belongs to God; human capacities in relation to God are zero."[95] Regrettably, this kind of theological thinking is not something that Wallace emphasizes.

In developing his imaginal approach to preaching, Wallace concentrates on Hillman's archetypal psychology. Hillman thinks of images as "manifestations of the soul."[96] Archetypal psychology works with its own particular understanding of soul. Most of us think of the soul as the innermost dimension of the self, that spiritual principle that animates us and produces our self-understanding. "But in the world of archetypal psychology, soul is identified not with spirit but with the sphere of psyche, and psyche is concerned with imagination and heart."[97] Care of the soul has to do with cultivating the images that arise out of our personal depths. Preachers, suggests Wallace, have the primary responsibility for caring for the images of the Judeo-Christian tradition. Stimulated by Hillman's thinking, he construes the preacher as someone who holds up the seminal images in the tradition in order to help people live "soul-full" lives through sermons that are "biblically grounded and experientially relevant."[98] Weaving gospel images is a powerful way to awaken the soul: "The preacher's responsible crafting of the images preserved in the biblical texts is one way to overturn the loss of soul found even in the world of religion. Through crafted images sown into the consciousness of a community, soul can be awakened, cultivated, and engaged."[99] Wallace turns to the archetypes associated with three Greek mythical characters—Apollo, Dionysius, and Hermes—to inform his imaginal preaching method. He notes that myth is the "primary rhetoric" of archetypal psychology.[100] The various mythic figures express the universal patterns that are innate to the psyche. The obvious objection to this approach is that it is inappropriate to use Greek mythology to inform a practice that is grounded in a Hebraic consciousness. Wallace responds in this way:

> I would propose that just as the great contribution of the Hebraic mind was to delineate the first and subsequent stirrings of the revelation of the God revealed in the experience of Israel and then

95. Craddock, "Preaching," 63.

96. Wallace, *Imaginal Preaching*, 22.

97. Ibid.

98. Ibid., 23.

99. Ibid., 34.

100. Ibid., 28.

most fully in Jesus of Nazareth and to provide in the books of the Bible an imaginal map of the reality of covenant with this God, so the contribution of Greek mythology was to offer one useful delineation of the various aspects of the human psyche through its figures of the gods and goddesses, charting the territory of the soul and naming its various ways of being in the world.[101]

The three mythic patterns are as follows. The Apollonian emphases, first, are order, balance, and harmony.[102] The Dionysian modalities are the feminine, the world of matter, and "mystical madness."[103] The Hermetic roles, lastly, are "the guide and messenger, the trickster and thief, the traveler and companion, the whisperer of night and day dreams."[104]

I appreciate very much the way in which Wallace brings the powerful tools of image, metaphor, and story to bear on the ministry of preaching. Indeed, these dynamics also feature in the approach that I am advocating. However, I am not convinced that it is either helpful or necessary to devote as much space (three chapters) as Wallace does to the Apollonian, Dionysian, and Hermetic modalities. These mythic figures manifest universal psychic patterns. The stories around them point up in a most vivid way fundamental human psychic tendencies, strengths, and weaknesses. One could just as easily study the characters of the Bible to find these same universal patterns. This is certainly not a plea for a Bible-only approach. As I indicated in the introduction, I am a strong supporter of the correlational approach in which the Christian heritage and creative cultural self-interpretations are brought into a mutually enriching conversation. My point is simply that the extended exploration into the mythic modalities that Wallace undertakes, as fascinating as it is in places, seems not to add very much to our understanding of the human psyche.

After surveying Wallace's sermons it is very evident that he is very gifted in the art of crafting a liturgical address. I found myself being very engaged, uplifted, and challenged by his sermons. Nonetheless, I feel compelled to register a concern over the way he sometimes uses his images. Wallace avers that "one can move to crafting a homily that features the images of the text while allowing them to be reworked by one's own

---

101. Ibid., 29.

102. Ibid., 63.

103. Ibid., 84.

104. Ibid., 102.

imagination and amplified by the images of one's own experience."[105] He takes full advantage of the hermeneutic liberty that this sentence expresses. It seems that sometimes he allows his imagination to run quite a distance from the text that he is preaching on. The sermon that particularly stands out for me in this regard is based on the gospel passage in which the angel rolls the stone away from the tomb (Matt 28:1–10). Wallace's theme is this: "The rock is whatever prevents us from entering the tomb, from dying and being buried with Christ." Below is an extract from the sermon:

> What is my stone? Our stone?
> Secrets that keep us nailed to a cross.
> Secret abuse we perform or tolerate or ignore.
> Secret judgments on which we build our lives, judgments that
> size up, diminish, and dismiss others.
> Secret hatreds and prejudices . . .[106]

This is certainly a creative approach. The image of the stone that blocks the way to Easter life is indeed a powerful one. The sermon would surely have engaged the congregation (or at least as many of them as any good preacher can expect) and perhaps even led to a significant transformation in some of them. The problem is that the image of the rock that blocks our way to Christlike living is simply not what the passage is about. Matthew is not proclaiming a message of conversion from vices but rather of the good news that this Jesus who died is now alive. Responsible preaching requires working with the images that are suggested by the central message of the text. Using one's imagination to spin off whatever image grabs one's interest or seems likely to have traction with the congregation is not appropriate. This takes us back to the Fosdickian approach and to one of its major weaknesses. One of Fosdick's sermons uses a very similar imagistic strategy to Wallace's. It is entitled, "The Means Determine the End," and the passage he works with is the story recorded in John's gospel of Jesus and the woman at the well (John 4:1–26).[107] Fosdick uses the verse, "Sir, you have nothing to draw with and the well is deep" to make his points. The image that he continually holds up for his listeners is the lack of a metaphorical bucket and rope to reach down to life-giving water. His theme is that to reach a worthy end one needs to employ a quality means. Links are made with marriage: You cannot get "lovely homes by unlovely means or faithful

---

105. Ibid., 71.

106. Ibid., 72.

107. See Fosdick, *Living Under Tension*, 102–11.

homes by unfaithful methods."[108] This is seen as an example of "Sir, you have nothing to draw with and the well is deep." A connection is also made with parenting. Parents too often do not take the time and effort to master the means to reach the ends they desire for their children. They make the mistake of loving their children for training them. It is necessary, says Fosdick, to face the critical issue in all areas of practical living of "how to." Finally, he reflects on the spiritual means needed to reach down into the well of God's grace and mercy. As with Wallace's rock, the bucket and rope (or the lack thereof) is used very creatively and no doubt those privileged to hear these sermons were significantly helped by them. Nevertheless, the value of staying close to the text should not be lost sight of. The preacher who is committed to letting the text speak for itself rather than mining it for a preachable image, will not give herself the license that Wallace and Fosdick have demonstrated in their approach in these sermons.

That completes our survey of the major voices in the area of the integration of preaching and counseling. In the conclusion to the chapter, I identify some principles drawn from this discussion that present as important in developing a sound model of therapeutic preaching.

Conclusion

There are a number of important principles pertaining to theocentric therapeutic preaching that have emerged from this historical survey of the dialogue between preaching and counseling. A fundamental principle is the essential affinity between preaching and counseling (Switzer, Capps, and Nichols). Some of those who take a narrative approach to preaching contend that the introduction of non-theological disciplines into the sermon is inappropriate. This strategy is viewed as importing an alien element. The work of the structuralists shows to the contrary that the basic aims and strategies associated with counseling are also found in preaching. Capps' work is particularly important here. He shows that far from there being antipathy between therapeutic and homiletical diagnosis of the human condition, there is actually correlation.

The second important insight has to do with the essential nature and function of a sermon. Preaching is not about supplying troubled souls with a weekly dose of psychological therapy (Switzer's objection). Preaching is a liturgical naming of the grace and mercy of God expressed through Christ

108. Ibid., 104.

in the power of the Holy Spirit. Psychology and counseling theory/practice should not therefore dominate a sermon. Rather, these resources should be used, when it is appropriate, as an aid to a vital, newsworthy expression of the beauty and power of the divine *therapeia*. Image and metaphor are powerful instruments for the task of proclamation of God's redemptive love and grace (Wimberly and Wallace). Psychology and counseling theory supply us with fresh images of God that breathe new life into the preaching of the divine *therapeia*. However, we should not fall into the trap of thinking that the images and metaphors in and of themselves are the healing and transformative agents (Wallace gives this impression at certain points in his work). The Holy Spirit inspires the images at the point of sermon preparation, and the same Spirit uses them during the preaching event to reach into the hearts, minds, and souls of those who come into the sanctuary thirsty for living water and the bread of life.

The previous point leads into the next. Therapeutic preaching is not simply about providing excellent information and offering arresting images drawn from counseling theory; it is essentially a transformative exercise. As Fosdick saw so clearly, the preacher must aim, with full reliance on divine grace, to not only talk about peace or joy or reconciliation, but to bring about that which she proclaims. The process in which lives are made over begins, or is given fresh impetus, when the sermon facilitates an encounter with healing love and liberating grace.

Oden's theological perspective also makes a very helpful contribution. The ultimate ground of all therapeutic work is the gracious and restorative love of God. In using analogues drawn from counseling theory, it is vitally important that the preacher refrain from making statements that imply that God is like a therapist. The message she needs to communicate is that the effective therapist participates in God's healing love.

The next useful insight that emerges is the importance of entering the internal frame of reference of the listeners (Capps). In Fosdick's colorful expression, preachers need to be "clairvoyant." The great preacher had an uncanny knack of zeroing in on the real needs of the members of his congregation. It is regrettable that Fosdick too often made the mistake of using a text as simply a leaping off point for his message. It is possible to let the meaning of the text unfold while still making clear and strong connections with one's listeners and their needs.

The final principle follows on from the last point. It is inappropriate to come with a psychologically informed message in hand in search of a passage to hang it off. The point of departure is an honest, open, and receptive engagement with the text that one is working with. The text must be allowed to speak for itself. If it seems that counseling theory can be used to bring a fresh perspective without distorting or misrepresenting the text, it is legitimate to draw it in. The correct approach is *therapeia* as servant of *kerygma*.

These are important principles for the job of developing an adequate model of therapeutic preaching. It is to the task of outlining such a model that we now turn.

2

The Model in Outline

IN OUTLINING THE MODEL of therapeutic preaching developed in this book, it is well to begin by defining the central terms. As was indicated above, references to therapeutic preaching in the literature are often negative. It is described as an approach to preaching in which the story of God's redemptive love in the encounter with Israel and with all of humanity through Christ is pushed to the margins and the narrative of psychological self-help is drawn into the center. Some will therefore be wondering why a term with negative connotations is employed here. I actually like the expression. A therapeutic act is one that brings healing, comfort, and relief. Life, it goes without saying, is often really hard. At certain points, we get buffeted about by the challenges that life hurls at us and it is all that we can do to hang on. In these times, words of understanding, encouragement, and help from the pulpit are eagerly and gratefully received. My understanding of therapeutic preaching encompasses healing and comfort, but it is also broader than this. Therapeutic work in a Christian context should not be conceived in narrowly psychological terms. Properly construed, it involves not only helping people with psychological growth and healing, but also challenging them (in a sensitive and respectful way) to grow into their God-given moral and spiritual potential. The way in which I interpret therapeutic preaching grows out of the model of pastoral counseling that I developed in my first book, *The Art of Listening*.[1] There I argued that while pastoral counseling is certainly concerned with helping persons cope with various psychological, existential, and developmental challenges, it is also focussed

1. Pembroke, *The Art of Listening*.

on challenging them to shape their lives in conformity to Christ. Similarly, therapeutic preaching needs this dual focus.

Human *therapeia* in this broad sense is an echo of divine *therapeia*. In the most general terms, God's healing love as it is presented in the story of Israel and of Jesus has two major thrusts. God reaches out with compassion, understanding, and forgiveness, but God also confronts the skewed values, distorted thinking, and destructive actions of God's people. In a word, God's therapy is expressed through both comfort and help, on the one hand, and challenge and confrontation, on the other.

Another important term used in my model is "theocentric." Some will contend that the term is redundant. Preaching is by definition a liturgical announcement of the grace of God in Christ. How could it be anything else but theocentric? While this is true in theory, the practice of many preachers represents a different story. One of the common complaints from homileticians is that the preaching they hear is not theological enough. By this they do not mean to say that there are too few references in sermons to Karl Barth and Jürgen Moltmann, to Elizabeth Johnson and Kathryn Turner. Rather, they mean that too much time in sermons is devoted to people and too little to God. This is particularly true of the preachers who major in psychological self-help. Human distress and psychological solutions dominate their sermons. The proposition that I put in this book is that a renewed model of therapeutic preaching puts God in Christ at the center of the sermon. The central thrust of this form of preaching is to open people more fully to divine *therapeia*.

The next essential feature of the approach to therapeutic preaching that I am proposing is the use of counseling theory to provide fresh images of God; these images are used to breathe new life into the proclamation of divine therapy. Some will protest that introducing a non-theological element into preaching constitutes a contamination of God's Word. That is, counseling theory is viewed as an alien factor. The work of the structuralists (Switzer, Capps, and Nichols) discussed in the last chapter makes an important contribution at this point. It demonstrates that there is an essential affinity between preaching and counseling. The basic aims and strategies associated with counseling are also part of pulpit ministry. There is no good reason, therefore, to view counseling theory as alien to preaching.

What is being proposed is a correlational approach. Correlation is, of course, a controversial method in theology. Many of the influential voices in modern theology have in fact been correlationalists. One need only think of theologians such as Friedrich Schleiermacher, Rudolph Bultmann, Paul Tillich, Karl Rahner, Jürgen Moltmann, David Tracy, Rosemary Radford Ruether, and Sally McFague. But opposition has come from some equally influential theologians. In the anti-correlation camp we find thinkers such as Karl Barth, Hans Frei, George Lindbeck, Stanley Hauerwas, and William Willimon. The nub of the issue is as follows. The correlationists contend that the use of psychology or philosophy allows us to grasp an important aspect of God's Word that would otherwise remain hidden. That is, when we approach the Bible with a relevant cultural self-interpretation in hand we see more than we saw before. The narrativists, on the other hand, argue that the use of a correlational approach inevitably means that the story of the Bible is forced into a preconceived pattern. That is, the biblical story gets fitted into another world with another story (the story that psychology or philosophy tells). In the context of my work here, I take the concerns of the narrativists very seriously. There is a very real danger that as soon as a preacher begins to make connections between the text and a particular psychological theory, she will start to manipulate the theological message to align with that theory. I have opted for a correlational approach because I make the judgment that the risk is worth taking. Provided one approaches the text honestly and with discipline, and provided one is judicious in the selection of the counseling theory that is employed, the correlational work will be legitimate. Moreover, it will produce valuable insights that would not otherwise have been available. In the end, the truth or otherwise in my contention is a matter of judgment. The reader will form her or his own view upon reviewing the sample sermons that are offered in chapter 6 as to whether insight or distortion is the result that is achieved.

The type of correlational work proposed in the model has a particular shape: counseling theory is used to fund metaphors for and analogues to divine *therapeia*. It is often assumed that "metaphor" and "analogy" can be used interchangeably. While there is overlap in the meaning of the terms, they can also be clearly distinguished. Metaphor is meaning-making, whereas analogy is explanatory. Metaphors are non-logical; analogies are logical. The fact that metaphors are non-logical means that they produce a twist in the semantic field. There is a logical opposition between the idea and its image. Consider the theological metaphor, God is light. It is the semantic impertinence or clash that is set up through referring to an infinite spiritual being as a source of illumination that gives the metaphor its power. It is precisely this logical opposition that is absent in analogy.

Analogy has more than one form, but if we take the most common one—namely, proportional analogy (ana-logon means "according to proper proportion")—which has the structure a:b as c:d, we will see immediately that this is the case. Using this analogical structure, we can say that God's righteousness (a) is to evil (b) as light (c) is to a dark place (d). There is no semantic impertinence here; rather, what we have is a logical explanation of the (strange) claim that God is light.

While metaphors may be useful in therapeutic preaching, the main burden of the figurative work is on analogy. For example, in the sample sermon on the prodigal son provided in chapter 6, use is made of the metaphor, "the mirroring God." "Mirroring" is the term coined by Heinz Kohut to describe the approving, confirming, admiring attitude of the therapist. Kohut found it particularly useful in working with shame-prone persons. He chose it because it captures the stance of the loving parent who mirrors or reflects back the joy and satisfaction that her child expresses upon doing something he is proud of. While employing this unusual way of referring to God serves to arrest attention—a valuable gain for any preacher!—to simply leave the congregation with this metaphor would not be particularly helpful. It is the explanation of it through analogical work that is the really important feature of the preaching. The aim is to express is a fresh and engaging way the beautiful truth that when we are struggling with shame feelings we can turn to the God who accepts and confirms us.

As indicated in the introduction, when it comes to analogical theology, the two approaches that feature are *analogia entis* and *analogia fidei*. In the style of therapeutic preaching that I propose, the analogy of faith is primary, but there is a very definite role assigned to the analogy of being. Preaching the divine *therapeia* takes its lead from *analogia fidei* (faithful proclamation of the divine *therapeia* through qualified words—words that bear a likeness to the divine reality to which they point), but it also incorporates *analogia entis* (reference to human therapeutic virtues gives us a revealing glimpse—and it is no more than that—of God's healing love, compassion, and acceptance).

There are two other important principles associated with responsible analogical theology in the context of preaching. It is necessary, first, to recognize that while analogical theology reveals similarity in the relation between humanity and God, it reveals an even greater dissimilarity. The profound otherness of God is acknowledged and respected in responsible analogical God-talk. In the context of therapeutic preaching, this means that while similarities between human and divine therapy are presented, the listener needs to be reminded that God's healing ways are as far above those of the therapists as the heavens are above the earth.

The other important principle—namely, that primacy in the analogical relation is properly with God—we have already hinted at. God has all the perfections (love, goodness, mercy, justice) perfectly and originally; we have them only imperfectly and derivatively. In the particular case of therapy, God's gracious and restorative love is the ground of human healing work. Thus, the compassion, acceptance, and empathy shown by a therapist are but faint echoes of what is expressed by God in Christ.

It is hoped that the main features of the model are now clear. In the next three chapters, these features will be discussed in much greater detail. Above it was suggested that authentic therapeutic preaching is theocentric. In the next chapter, important and influential approaches to locating God in Christ at the center of the sermon will be surveyed.

3

God in Christ at the Center of the Sermon

IN THE FIRST CHAPTER, a number of critical appraisals of Harry Emerson Fosdick's approach to preaching as counseling on a group scale were identified. We saw that Lee Ramsey objects that "constant attention in preaching to the particular needs of the hearers . . . obscures the truth that God's answer to human suffering is already and ever again given in Christ."[1] We also noted that Mike Graves laments the fact that too often preachers adopting a therapeutic approach fail to point their hearers to God's redeeming love. The focus is on human behavior; people get placed at the center of the sermon. "We forget, grammatically speaking, that even if the *object* of our proclamation . . . is to speak a relevant word to our listeners, God remains the *subject*."[2] To give one last example, Tom Long contends that for Fosdick the real interest and action in preaching is using the gospel to solve personal problems, when it is really about giving the news that because of what happened in the Christ event life can never be the same again.[3] For Long, all Christian preaching is "a reverberation of the Easter kerygma."[4] In sum, the problem that these three scholars identify is that people and their needs rather than God in Christ is established as the frame of reference in this kind of preaching.

Those who engage in therapeutic preaching do have a tendency—and it's a strong one—to locate human problems and psychological answers to

---

1. Ramsey, *Care-full Preaching*, 16.
2. Graves, "God of Grace," 110 (emphasis in the original).
3. Long, "No News," 150.
4. Ibid., 149.

those problems at the center of the sermon. An important principle in my approach is that the central point of reference of therapeutic preaching is God's healing love. The primary source of healing that is named in preaching needs to be the divine *therapeia*.

Given that the Bible as a whole tells the story of God's saving work in human history, and that the central focus in the Christian Scriptures is God's reconciling work in and through the cross and resurrection of Christ, one might be forgiven for thinking that there is no need to remind preachers of what they should be preaching about. However, it is instructive to observe the experience of Paul Scott Wilson in teaching homiletics to his students over many years.[5] Wilson sensed that something was missing in the sermons he was hearing, but he couldn't put his finger on it. The students preached from the Bible, carried out solid exegesis, applied the texts to the contemporary context, used vivid images and metaphors, and addressed important ethical, social justice, and pastoral issues. Despite all these important boxes being checked, there was one left unchecked. Eventually he found this box: "Perhaps I simply assumed that when the Bible was in the sermon, God was the subject. It slowly dawned on me that people were the main focus, and the reason many sermons had no power was that God was largely absent."[6]

In seeking to show why God in Christ needs to be at the center in responsible preaching, I could add to the works already cited ones by any number of important contemporary homileticians. The approach I take, however, is not one of surveying this illustrious group and lifting out the bits that support my proposal. Rather, I attend to this theme as it is represented in three major theological schools—namely, neo-orthodoxy, the new hermeneutic, and postliberalism. The reason that I have taken this line is not because I consider that the way in which the various theologians chosen for attention frame the issue is necessarily superior to that of the likes of Graves, Long, Wilson, Craddock, Buttrick, and Willimon. I have taken this approach because, along with offering important and influential perspectives on God in Christ at the center of the sermon, the discussion raises in a vivid way an issue that is crucial in the context of my approach to therapeutic preaching, viz., the legitimacy or otherwise of correlation between the Christian symbols and contemporary cultural insights. The reader will note that some of the theologians surveyed use a correlational

5. Wilson, *Setting Words on Fire*, xii.
6. Ibid., xii.

approach, while others object to this method. The chapter concludes with a preliminary attempt to address the issue of correlational preaching. An argument is made—in outline at least—for the validity of, and value in, integrating insights from the psychotherapeutic domain into a sermon.

I should also make the point that in attending to the work of the representatives in the three schools, it will be evident that there are a number of contentious issues associated with the way in which they construct their theology of preaching. However, my concern is not with adjudicating on the merits or otherwise of the various theological positions. Rather, my intention is to show that when the various insights and arguments are taken together, the case for locating God in Christ at the center of the sermon is overwhelming. Now that the context for the chapter has been set, we turn to the first of our schools—namely, neo-orthodoxy.

Neo-Orthodox Approaches

I have selected for treatment here two leading (and quite different) voices in the neo-orthodox school—namely, Karl Barth and Rudolph Bultmann. In his introduction to his collection of Barth's early sermons, William Willimon tells us that his image of the young preacher at Safenwil is of him "whooping it up in the pulpit, pouring forth a torrent of metaphor mixed with questions and declarations, in fits and starts, lurching from left to right but always with *vision focused exclusively upon the God who is rendered in the Scripture*."[7] When I was scanning through my mental files searching for theologians to turn to in developing the picture of a tradition in which God in Christ is located very definitely at the center of the sermon, Karl Barth was the first to pop up. Rudolph Bultmann is equally strong in his conviction about what properly belongs in the center of the preaching frame. Bultmann sees the task of the preacher as proclaiming Christ as lord of the new age that began with his death and resurrection. However, the way he understands the Easter proclamation is quite different to Barth. For Bultmann, the mythological categories the New Testament uses in speaking about the cross and the resurrection need to be reinterpreted. It is only when they are rendered in existentialist language that they become meaningful for modern persons. In essence, the kerygma has the function of leading a person into genuine existential self-understanding.

7. Barth, *Early Preaching of Barth*, xvii (emphasis added).

Karl Barth

At the forefront of Barth's thinking when he began to develop his theological system was what he saw as the fundamental error in the approach of the liberal theologians of the nineteenth century. That error was to place human questions and answers on center stage. The rightful position of God was usurped; God was pushed off to the wings.

In his theology, Barth relentlessly insists on the primacy of God in the divine-human relation. The starting point and the finishing point in any theological inquiry is always God in Christ. The Bible is not primarily concerned about right human thoughts about God; its major focus is right divine thoughts about humanity.[8] The question of the Scriptures is not how we should speak about God, but rather what God has to say to us. The Bible is not so much interested in how we can find our way to God, but in how God has sought us out and found God's way to us. The central message in the Hebrew and Christian Scriptures is not the way in which we can put ourselves in right relationship to God, but of a covenant relationship that God established first with Abraham, Moses, and David, and in a definitive manner in and through the death and resurrection of Christ.

When Barth approaches the issue of proclamation in the church, his starting point is that the focus needs to be not on pressing human questions—our suffering, our sin, our doubt, our mortality—but on the question that God poses.[9] According to him, the Bible that we preach from refers these concerns in a primary way to God. In the biblical perspective, we suffer because of God; we sin against God; our doubt is doubt of God; our living and our dying is determined by God. The central question is the one that confronts us in the cross of Christ. "The cross is the demand of God that we ask about him, about God: it is his declaration that as long as we live, though all other questions may finally be answered, we may not tear ourselves loose from *this* one."[10]

In the Bible, our questions are translated into the question that cannot be side-stepped—namely, the question about God. In attending to the question, one necessarily hears the answer. When God questions us, God's answer is not "a great No."[11] It is true that God does say "No," but God's

---

8. Barth, *Word of God*, 43.

9. Ibid., 116.

10. Ibid., 119.

11. Ibid., 120.

final word is "Yes." God speaks a word of judgment, but the last word is grace. We are dead in our sin, but alive in Christ. Christ was crucified, but God spoke a great word of affirmation through the resurrection.

The preacher needs to be the first to submit to God's question and to hear God's answer. Her role is not to reflect on the people's many questions and to answer them from the Bible. She needs to sit under God's questioning, to take in God's answer, and in this way to proclaim a message that shows the people where they need to be looking. God determines what questions are the really important ones; the responsibility of the preacher is to expose the people to God's questioning—something that she herself has entered into first. "[B]eing truly questioned by God and truly questioning about God, [the preacher] will know God's answer and so be able to give it to the people, who with *their* question really want *God's* answer, even though they do not realize it."[12]

Another name for God's question, which is at the same time God's answer, is the Word of God. Barth refers to the threefold form of the Word of God: The Word of God preached, the Word of God written, and the Word of God revealed (the Word became flesh).[13] Preaching for Barth is essentially the intention to speak the Word of God Himself (the third form and ground of the other two forms). He refers to the Word of God Himself as the "center," "the point of reference" to which proclamation is oriented.[14] What the Word of God has to say is the decisive factor in preaching, but he cannot say it directly. Preaching involves an interaction between God's Word and human words. However, primacy is absolutely with the former. This is made clear by Barth in his decision in *Homiletics* to define preaching through two formulas:

1. Preaching is the Word of God which he himself speaks, claiming for the purpose the exposition of a biblical text in free human words that are relevant to contemporaries by those who are called to do this in the church that is obedient to its commission.

2. Preaching is the attempt enjoined upon the church to serve God's own Word, through one who is called thereto, by expounding a biblical text in human words and making it relevant to contemporaries in intimation of what they have to hear from God himself.[15]

12. Ibid., 123.
13. Barth, *Church Dogmatics* I.1 §4.
14. Ibid., 59.
15. Barth, *Homiletics*, 44.

In this way Barth acknowledges that preaching is service of God's Word involving the preacher's own words, but the way the formulas are framed makes it absolutely clear that primacy is with God's speech. The opening phrase is, "Preaching is the Word of God which he himself speaks." He then goes on to state that God uses human words to declare God's message. The faithful preacher is the one who knows that she is simply the mouthpiece of the divine message. "Proclamation is human speech in and by which God Himself speaks like a king through the mouth of his herald, and which is meant to be heard and accepted as speech in and by which God Himself speaks . . ."[16] For this reason, Barth prefers the word "announcement" to "proclamation."[17] The decisive fact is that it is God who speaks; the preacher simply has the role of announcing what God wants to say.

If preaching is nothing more or less than announcing God's creative and redemptive work, then it follows that it must not attempt to do the work of God. Barth reflects on the different understandings that certain people have concerning the task of preaching.[18] Some people, for example, say that the sermon should be directed at building up the kingdom of God. Others stress the importance of the preacher seeking to bring people to conversion, to a point of decision. Others simply say that preaching is about confronting people with the reality of God. Barth, for his part, avers that all these things may indeed happen in a sermon, but they are rightly seen as acts which God is prosecuting. They should not be seen as human tasks. The preacher serves *God's* purpose of building up the kingdom, of bringing people to a point of decision, of confronting people with sin and grace.

The central element in the divine work, and therefore in the divine address to us, is that God has come to us in Christ. "Behind the two formulas [in Barth's definition] there finally stands the decisive statement of Christology regarding the unity between God and us in Jesus Christ."[19] The content of preaching for Barth is the first and second advents. In *Homiletics*, Barth refers to these saving actions as the "unconditional whence" and the "unconditional whither."[20] The "whence" refers to the incarnation. God has revealed God's self in Jesus; the Word became flesh. The "last word" of this incarnation was spoken in Christ's action on the cross. In Christ, we have

---

16. Barth, *Church Dogmatics* I.1, 53.

17. See Barth, *Homiletics*, 45–46; idem, *Church Dogmatics* I.1, 60.

18. Barth, *Homiletics*, 48.

19. Ibid., 45.

20. Ibid., 51, 53.

been reconciled to God. Barth says that preaching has this "whence" as its central point of reference.

But preaching Christ is not simply a matter of saying the words "incarnation" and "Christ." Preaching is not the presentation of a concise summary of what God has done in Christ. It is not an act of description, but rather an event. "The concrete encounter of God and [humanity] today, whose actuality, of course, can be created by the Word of God Himself, must find a counterpart in the human event of proclamation . . ."[21]

Preachers, observes Barth, have a tendency to frame their sermons around human issues and struggles.[22] They talk, for example, about sin and errors in doctrine. They also like to focus on the need for holy living. They discuss what this entails and how to achieve it. The emphasis is on *our* sin, *our* errors, and *our* sanctification. What is too often overlooked, observes Barth, is that talk of sin, heresy, and sanctification needs to be set very firmly in the context of the "unconditional whence." Through the Word of God sin is forgiven, errors are corrected, and people are empowered to live holy lives.

Barth contends that the sermon must be equally concerned with the "unconditional whither."[23] The New Testament declares that in Christ the revelation, reconciliation, and fulfilment of God have taken place unconditionally and once and for all, but it also declares that these things are ahead of us no less unconditionally. Preaching draws a connecting line between Christ's first and second coming. The essence of the preacher's call is to stand between the two advents. "Like the Christ who has appeared already, the Christ who is still to come must be the center of every sermon. All that we say must be subordinate to this: Christ comes, we await his day."[24]

Rudolph Bultmann

Rudolph Bultmann's fundamental starting point in his theological program is that the mythic concepts and formulations found in the New Testament present as simply incredible to many modern people. They cannot believe in a cosmos with a three-story structure in which the world is the theater for the activities of various supernatural powers. A modern person typically cannot understand how spiritual entities can impact on an individual

21 Ibid., 53.

22. Ibid., 52.

23. Ibid., 53–54.

24. Ibid., 54.

and shape her spiritual life. She sees herself as responsible for her own existence. Her view of herself is of a self-contained, internally directed entity that is not open to supernatural engagement and influence by God and God's angels on the one side, and by Satan and his demons on the other.

With this in mind, Bultmann set about identifying the essential truths in the New Testament message that are not tied to the mythical world picture. His approach, however, was not one of eliminating the mythical elements. That is, it was not one of purifying the New Testament of elements such as the virgin birth, angels and demons, and an atoning sacrifice in order to get to the essential, non-mythic, core. Bultmann says that his work "is not a process of subtraction but a hermeneutical method."[25] It is his contention that myth should be interpreted in existentialist rather than cosmological terms. He finds in Heidegger's existentialist analysis a secular statement of the message of the New Testament.[26] Heidegger sees human existence as one which is essentially characterized by a basic anxiety and of care for self in that anxiety. The human person is gripped by a deep-seated anxiety arising from the fact that she must constantly choose the person she is. She lives in a moment of decision between the past and the future. She has the choice of either losing herself in the everyday world of things at hand (those things that we use in work and in leisure) or of attaining authenticity by opening herself fully to the future—and especially to death as the defining feature in that future.

Philosophy claims that it is able to identify both authentic and inauthentic forms of existence and thereby point the way to conversion. If we have knowledge of authenticity we are in a position to decide about ourselves and thus to direct the course of our personal development. Here Bultmann finds a decisive difference of perspective to that of the New Testament. According to the Gospel, human beings, in their pride and arrogance, convince themselves that they have the means at their disposal to justify themselves. The good news that God brings in Christ is the exposure of this illusion and the opening up of the way to authentic existence. This comes through radical self-renunciation and submission to God in obedient trust. Thus, authentic existence is not something that one can obtain through one's own efforts; it is something that comes as absolute gift. Sin and redemption are thereby rendered in non-mythological terms: "Talk about sin no longer seems mythological in the moment in which the love

25. Bultmann, "Problem of Demythologizing," 99.
26. Bultmann, "New Testament and Mythology," 22.

of God encounters us as the power that encompasses and upholds us, that upholds us even in our highhandedness and fallenness, that accepts us for what we are not, and thus frees us from ourselves as we are."[27]

According to Bultmann, modern people cannot be expected to believe in the cross in terms of sacrifice and atonement for sin set in a cultic and juridical frame. Neither can they be expected to believe in the resurrection as God's supernatural act of resuscitating a dead corpse. The meaning of the Christ event is to be found in its power to liberate us from our prideful assumption that we can justify ourselves.[28] The New Testament proclamation is simply this: that which we cannot do, God has done, and is doing, for us in the cross and resurrection of Christ.

The central question for Bultmann is this: How does a person come to believe in the cross and resurrection as the salvation occurrence? He contends that there is only one answer: people come to such belief because the cross and resurrection of Christ are proclaimed. It is only in the preached word that Christ the crucified and risen one is encountered.[29] It for this reason that Bultmann could happily embrace a formula that was thrown at him as criticism, "Jesus has risen into the kerygma."[30]

It is therefore a mistake, according to Bultmann, to attempt to get back behind the proclamation to establish its historical origin—as if such an investigation could legitimate the Christ event. The word of the cross that is proclaimed is God's word to us. We are simply asked whether or not we are prepared to make the Easter faith our own. When this word comes to us we are drawn into an eschatological frame. That is, we are drawn into a moment of decision in which we must choose between living in the old age and embracing the new one that has dawned in and through the cross and resurrection of Christ. Bultmann avers that the content of preaching is the message that Christ is lord of the new era.[31]

Those who are stuck in the old era are "living in the flesh."[32] The domain of the flesh encompasses everything that is visible, material, within our grasp, and therefore ours to use as we choose. It is the world that we claim as our own and construct according to our personal will and intention.

27. Ibid., 29.

28. Ibid., 30.

29. Ibid., 39.

30. Kay, *Preaching and Theology*, 43.

31. Bultmann, "Preaching," 241.

32. Bultmann, "New Testament and Mythology," 16.

It incorporates those things that we are able to achieve through our own efforts, including the "works of the law." Those who live according to the flesh are puffed up with pride and believe that their own righteousness is, like everything else, something that they themselves can achieve.

Christ the Lord calls us into the new era, the era of the Spirit.[33] Life in the Spirit is genuine human life, authentic existence. It is lived out of what is invisible and therefore not ours to grasp hold of and use. To live in this realm is to take up an attitude of surrender because here we have no control. Here there are no material things for us to take hold of and use to build up a (false) sense of security through our achievements. The life of the Spirit is received by grace through faith. Faith is "radical submission to God, which expects everything from God and nothing from ourselves; and it is the release thereby given from everything in the world that can be disposed of, and hence the attitude of being free from the world, of freedom."[34]

The task of the preacher, according to Bultmann, is to proclaim the Easter faith and, in so doing, to call the listeners to a moment of decision. They must decide whether they are going to live by the flesh or by the Spirit, whether they are going to remain bound by the illusions and false securities of the old age or be set free by the Lord of the new age. "True preaching is that which preaches Jesus Christ as Lord . . . Thus it is crucial that he be present as Lord in the preached word itself, and that where this word resounds the end of the world be present to the auditor, in that it places before him a decision, whether he will remain the old [person] or become the [new person]."[35]

The New Hermeneutic

Two former students of Rudolph Bultmann—namely, Gerhard Ebeling and Ernst Fuchs—were influential voices in the theological movement known as the new hermeneutic. Ebeling and Fuchs agree with their teacher that the call to decision is an essential feature of the kerygma. However, they contend that it is not possible to fully understand the content of the Easter message without recourse to a critical historical analysis of the person and message of Jesus. Such an historical quest is not simply about fact-finding. The task for the modern preacher is to use the results of the historical study

33. Ibid., 17.
34. Ibid., 18.
35. Bultmann, "Preaching," 242.

to "bring God to speech." That is, she must do more than simply provide a contemporary interpretation of Jesus and the kerygma. Her calling is to articulate the reality of Jesus' life, teaching, and cross/resurrection in such a way that her listeners are confronted with a decision concerning their way-of-being-in-the-world. When God is brought to speech, those who hear the message are challenged to take up the radical way of love of God and neighbor that Jesus preached about and expressed in the fullest possible way in his own mode of being.

Gerhard Ebeling

Ebeling agrees with Bultmann that the essence of preaching is the proclamation of the Christ event. That is, the kerygma is also the kerygma of Christ.[36] He uses the concept of word-event to describe the true nature of kerygmatic preaching. Preaching the kerygma means more than simply restating the message of salvation from sin and death through Christ's death and resurrection. That is, preaching is not simply providing information about the gospel; it is a word-event that recaptures something of the power of the original word-event that came into being in the person and work of Jesus. In order to understand what is meant by the concept of word-event, it is necessary to observe that words do not simply point to actions and decisions; they are the vehicles through which these things happen. As J. L. Austin saw so clearly, language is performative.[37] Language does not simply describe things, it *does* things. A vow is a case in point. When in a marriage service a woman says, "I, Jill, in the presence of God take you, Tom, to be my husband . . . as long as we both shall live," she is not giving information about a marriage vow, she is enacting it. Through the words she has spoken, she is committing herself in love to her husband for life. Ebeling puts it this way: "Word is, taken strictly, happening word. It is not enough to inquire into its intrinsic meaning, but that must be joined up with the question of its future, of what it effects."[38] The human's existence is actually a word-event—a word-event that has its origin in the Word of God. Because the ground of the speech-events that constitute us as human beings is God's Word, we are called to a response to that Word.

---

36. Ebeling, *Theology and Proclamation*, 32.

37. Austin, *How to Do Things*.

38. Ebeling, "Word of God," 103.

It is the call-response structure in preaching that makes it kerygmatic: "The kerygma considered as Word is an event which overtakes the [person] who hears it and forces him to a decision between faith and unfaith, and consequently to a decision about his own understanding of himself."[39]

The challenge for those who preach today, according to Ebeling, is that the christological titles (Jesus is the Christ, Jesus is Lord, Jesus is the Son of God) through which the kerygma is expressed are no longer meaningful for most modern persons. The preacher needs to interpret them for her listeners. This will necessitate a thoroughgoing historical study. But the aim is not to simply present interesting and illuminating information concerning how Jesus was understood by the earliest Christian community. What the preacher is trying to get at in her historical investigation is a grasp of the understanding of God and of human existence that is expressed in these titles. "Every christological title represents a particular interpretation of reality, and this means in concrete terms a particular understanding of the way in which [the human] is claimed, questioned, threatened, and given hope."[40] In other words, these titles are part of the word-event that is Christ. An interpretation of the titles has the potential to show us the true nature of human existence today, and thus to confront people with the claims that are expressed in them.

What is required today is a new interpretation of the traditional message that restores to the Word its event character. For this reason, Ebeling avers that it would be wrong to think that all that the modern preacher needs to do is to simply interpret the traditional kerygma for her listeners. The preacher's task is twofold: to bring a contemporary interpretation to the traditional message, and then, guided by this interpretation, to preach kerygmatically.[41] That is, to preach in a way that the claims of the kerygma are felt by the listeners. Put differently, proclamation involves setting up an encounter between the message and the listener, thereby demonstrating that this message is necessary for her in her quest for a meaningful and authentic existence.

Ultimately, the task for the preacher is to find that right word, the word that is true, necessary, liberating. Ebeling's approach to hermeneutics centers on the power of the word to bring illumination. It is the word that "opens

---

39. Ebeling, *Theology and Proclamation*, 41.

40. Ibid., 49–50.

41. Ibid., 53.

up and mediates understanding."⁴² That is, the problem facing the person seeking understanding is not that a particular verbal statement is obscure, but rather that the situation that it refers to lacks clarity. The preacher needs therefore the interpretive skills to illumine both the situation of Jesus, the message he preached, and the message preached about him, and, at the same time, the situation of the modern person. When she is successful in this task, she grasps the word "by means of which one [person] can speak God to another so that God comes to [humanity] and [humanity] to God."⁴³ The word-event has the nature of a promise.⁴⁴ A promise involves a pledge to bring something into existence. It is promised that that which is now absent will one day be present. In this way, a future is opened up for the person to whom the pledge has been made by awakening faith in her.

In the context of the gospel, the preacher prosecutes a word-event in which the love and grace of Christ are announced, thereby opening up a future—a future in God—for those who receive the word. "For God's word is not various things, but one single thing—the word that makes [a person] human by making him [or her] a believer, i.e., a [person] who confesses to God as his [or her] future and therefore does not fail [others] in the one absolutely necessary and salutary thing, viz., true word."⁴⁵

This way of speaking about the Word of God connects Ebeling with Bultmann's approach: the kerygma is that which calls for a decision for belief (or unbelief). What is different in Ebeling's perspective is that the person and message of Jesus is seen as having a vitally important role in relation to the kerygma. Ebeling observes that Bultmann was only concerned with the *that* of the kerygma. That is, for Bultmann the pursuit of a critical analysis of the person, words, and acts of the historical Jesus would contribute nothing to the proclamation of the kerygma. What is of prime importance is *that* God has acted in Christ. Because God has acted in Christ, those who hear this fact proclaimed are brought to a point of decision. For Ebeling, however, the *what* and the *how* are important. He asks this question: "How then can one avoid the impression, if the evaluation of Jesus in the kerygma remains unintelligible, that we are dealing with no more than an abstract mythogumenon?"⁴⁶ According to Ebeling,

42. Ebeling, "Word of God," 93.

43. Ibid., 104.

44. Ibid., 104–5.

45. Ibid., 105.

46. Ebeling, *Theology and Proclamation*, 39.

explicit christological kerygma (cross/resurrection as the salvific event) is founded on implicit christological kerygma (the person of Jesus himself).[47] For this reason, explicit christological kerygma that stands alone, that lacks the grounding that implicit christological kerygma provides, is empty:

> If we are not confronted with implicit christological kerygma, explicit christological kerygma remains utterly void, without authority, without reality. Implicit christological kerygma is the word-event in which the encounter with Jesus brings God to expression in the reality which we live. It is the word-event where God is brought to expression in such a way that this confrontation leads to the basis of faith . . .[48]

The essential task for the modern preacher is to interpret both implicit and explicit christological statements for those who have lost contact with them. However, the way in which she does this must have the character of a word-event. The listener needs to hear the Word addressing him or her, calling for decision.

Ernst Fuchs

Fuchs's approach to a theology of proclamation also centers on word-event—or, as he prefers, "speech-event."[49] In describing what he means by this term, Fuchs begins by observing that every act of speech has a particular content. Further, this content has a history. At a certain point in time prior to a conversation that is currently taking place, the speaker had a particular view of the subject that she is now speaking about. But that view may well have changed. In fact, let us assume that it has. In this situation, what has taken place is that she has been confronted with new information, with new ideas, arguments, and perspectives. That is, she has been brought to a point of decision. She has been forced to decide whether she will stick with her old view, or move to a new one on the basis of the new information that has come into her possession. The moment of decision has brought unity to the diversity of perspectives that she has been grappling with. "This power of speech which creates unity," says Fuchs, "is what I call

---

47. Ibid., 77.
48. Ibid., 79.
49. Fuchs, "Proclamation and Speech-Event."

the 'speech-event.'"[50] When she communicates the content that has been formed in this way she discloses her "situation." She offers to the other person her view of herself, of life, of God. In this way, she is sharing her being. It is the engagement in which there is an interaction (either confirming or challenging in nature) between the situation—the situation that discloses a distinct manner of being—of two or more people that constitutes what Fuchs calls a speech-event:

> The real content of speech, that which is event not only in speech but also precisely as speech among [persons], is therefore being-itself. But because being-itself discloses in speech something like our situation, as that which is ever and again understood between us, I term being-itself *"situation."* Situation is the essence of the "speech-event."[51]

We saw above that Ebeling contended against Bultmann that the *what* and the *how* of Jesus are as important as the *that*. Fuchs shares this view. The kerygma on the one hand, and the person and message of Jesus on the other, need to be set in dialogue: "Jesus illuminates the apostles' talk and their talk illuminates Jesus' task. *This is why I have in my own way renewed the question of the historical Jesus.*"[52] In attempting to understand Jesus more fully, Fuchs construes Jesus' proclamation as a speech-event. He claims that in the parables Jesus' understanding of his situation "'comes to speech' in a special way."[53] What Jesus is attempting to do, the way in which he sees his "situation," is to call people to a point of decision. The context for this decision is time.[54] Jesus announces a new time. Indeed, the time is now. Now is the time to receive the future God offers those who come in faith. In the parables, Jesus announces to his listeners that there is an immensely precious future on offer (a "treasure," a "pearl of great price"). In short, he is proclaiming a new situation for them. In this new way-of-being-in-the-world, a person gives herself fully in love to God and to others—even to her enemies. Jesus used the parables as a means to "bring God to speech."[55]

---

50. Ibid., 349.

51. Ibid., 349–50.

52. Fuchs, "New Testament and Hermeneutical Problem," 136 (emphasis in the original).

53. Fuchs, "Proclamation," 348.

54. Fuchs, "The New Testament and Hermeneutical Problem," 129.

55. Fuchs, "Proclamation," 348.

The task for preaching today is to likewise bring God "to speech." In the earliest form of preaching, the one who proclaimed became the proclaimed. Jesus' own person moved to the center of the kerygma. Jesus is the one who was faithful to God in accepting the cross, and whom God exalted by raising him to life. Jesus now becomes central in speech about God:

> [N]o one can speak of God if he intends somehow to do this and still by-pass Jesus. Jesus therefore became the text of the proclamation. But the written word does not replace the proclamation. It simply preserves the *situation* in which one has to speak of God. One has to speak of God in that Jesus himself is proclaimed as Word of God; in such a way that faith in God sets free the speech-power which is presented to it, and with this power faith is able to speak of Jesus, because it has understood him.[56]

On this view, the renewal of preaching needs to start with a retrieval of the speech-event that came to expression in Jesus. It is only as contemporary preachers are able to grasp the situation of Jesus and the way in which he brought God to speech as the one who graciously offers a new way of being in which a person is freed to love God and neighbor that they authentically proclaim the gospel. Contemporary speech about God that is connected to the tradition of Jesus will lead listeners to a point of decision. It is the call to decision that Fuchs sees as the essential feature of Jesus' parables. The essence of the decision is this: Am I content to continue in my current, lost situation, or can I find the courage to respond in faith to the call of the Lord of life who is offering the possibility of becoming a new creation?

Postliberal Approaches

Leading proponents of the new homiletic such as Fred Craddock and Eugene Lowry drew significantly on the insights of Ebeling and Fuchs. In particular, they sought to apply a central concept in the new hermeneutic—namely, the word-event. Craddock, for example, observes that for the biblical writers the Word is viewed not simply as a fund of knowledge; it is construed first and foremost as performative: it does things. When the Word is spoken an encounter between God and humanity is enacted. In *As One Without Authority*, Craddock avers that it is wrong to privilege God's acts over God's speech. Word and act are indissolubly linked:

56. Ibid., 353–54.

> Let those who oppose the preaching ministry with phrases such as "the acts of God" and "salvation events" recall the role of spoken words within those events that gave their character and the role of spoken words in sharing the benefits of those events. There is in our experience no event so profound as speaking one with another.[57]

The preached word makes something happen. It creates an experience of the love, grace, and judgment of God. In *Doing Time in the Pulpit*, Eugene Lowry also works with this idea. The method that preachers need to adopt is one in which there is shift from ideas to experience.[58] Preaching that simply presents ideas and concepts does not do justice to God's Word. God's Word is a living, moving, transforming entity. That is, when the Word is spoken truly it comes to people with transformative power. In his work on preaching informed by the postliberal theology of Hans Frei,[59] Charles Campbell takes issue with this understanding of the Word as primarily generative of religious experience. It is to this work that we now turn.

Charles Campbell

Campbell accepts, of course, that God's Word can and does move people. His concern with the approach of Craddock, Lowry, and others associated with the new homiletic is the heavy emphasis that is assigned to the role of the Word in creating an experience. Campbell suggests that these homileticians have not paid sufficient attention to the fact that God can act through the preached word without moving people. Moreover, he is concerned that this approach puts human experience rather than God at the center of the sermon. "As Frei would put it," writes Campbell, "the emphasis on experience brings with it the danger of theological 'relationalism'—a relationalism that dares to make no claims for God apart from the experience of human beings. Human experience becomes the focus of the sermon, rather than God in Jesus Christ . . ."[60]

Along these lines, Campbell is critical of the way in which Craddock construes preaching as essentially reflection on ordinary human experience from the perspective of the gospel. (We note that for Craddock, such reflection

---

57. Craddock, *One without Authority*, 36.

58. Lowry, *Time in the* Pulpit, 13.

59. Campbell, *Preaching Jesus*.

60. Ibid., 141.

needs to make use of evocative images.) This understanding of proclamation comes through in a number of places in *As One without Authority*:

> By means of images the preaching occasion will be a re-creation of the way life is experienced now held under the light of the gospel.[61]

> Simply put, this task [the task for the inductive preacher] is to use evocative imagery that will allow the congregation to see and hear what she has seen and heard. What she has seen and heard is not a special esoteric corpus of information about God that has been delivered to her to pass along, but our existence as it is in the liberating light of God's graciousness toward us.[62]

Campbell contends that in this understanding of preaching, "Jesus becomes too easily a cipher for human experience and in the process can virtually evaporate as a unique identity who 'turns to us.'"[63] Let me say in passing that it is difficult to see how Craddock is elevating human experience at the expense of the gospel. His aim, rather, is to encourage preachers to cast the images that have emerged from their engagement with the text with the requisite power needed to effect necessary changes in the attitudes and values that shape the way-of-being-in-the-world of their parishioners.[64] In a word, Craddock is making a plea for preaching the Word that has the power to transform lives. It is difficult to see how this is possible in the absence of some reflection on the way human existence is commonly lived today. Craddock is not seeking to elevate human experience, to shift the focus from Jesus to human beings; he simply wants to set our typical patterns of existence in dialogue with the gospel. In general terms, this approach aligns with the one that I take in this book. However it may be in relation to Campbell's critique of the inductive method, the important thing for our purposes is his focus on "preaching Jesus." Such preaching attends to "the unique, unsubstitutable identity of Jesus as the ascriptive subject of his own predicates."[65]

Here Campbell is drawing on central technical terms employed by Frei in his book, *The Identity of Jesus*.[66] The "ascriptive logic" that Frei refers

61. Craddock, *One without Authority*, 65.

62. Ibid., 74.

63. Campbell, *Preaching Jesus*, 142.

64. Craddock, *One without Authority*, 75.

65. Campbell, *Preaching Jesus*, 142.

66. Frei, *Identity of Jesus*.

to consists of the grammatical assertion that Jesus is the subject of his own predicates. That is, the predicates applied to Jesus cannot be arrived at by a process of abstraction that is funded by an analysis of a collection of Gospel texts. A proper understanding of Jesus' identity is arrived at by careful attention to the way in which the Gospel story depicts his intentions and actions. Speaking generally, one finds an answer to the question, What is this person like? by attending to what he or she typically does. Thus, it is not the statement "Jesus is love" that is of primary significance, but rather the way in which Jesus uniquely enacts love in the Gospel story.

Jesus' enactment of love is intimately connected to the coexistence of power and powerlessness.[67] There are two facets—two facets that are indissolubly linked—to the unique way in which Jesus expresses love. On the one hand, there is Jesus' obedient love for the Father; on the other, his love for humankind. In obedience to God, Jesus consents to powerlessness: "Yet not what I want, but what you want" (Mark 14:36). This transition to helplessness constitutes his unique identity. The story of salvation is one in which Jesus identifies with the helplessness of the guilty. Yet this helplessness is his salvific power. In becoming helpless he shows the full power of his love and obedience. The history-like story of the gospel, unlike myth, is not an expression of certain aspects of universal human experience. Rather, this story renders the identity of a particular person whose life, death, and resurrection enacted God's saving will for the world. With this in mind, Campbell contends that "preaching should adhere to the ascriptive logic of the gospels and dare to preach Jesus of Nazareth in all his particularity by rendering him as the subject of his own predicates."[68]

Mark Ellingsen

Like Charles Campbell, Mark Ellingsen is guided in his approach to preaching by the postliberal theology of Hans Frei and George Lindbeck. In keeping with this perspective, Ellingsen interprets biblical literature as history-like, realistic narrative. Accordingly, questions of historicity and scientific criticism are secondary. The narratives should be approached in terms of literary principles and logic. The role of the preacher is to tell the story from within its own frame of reference: "It is sufficient that we simply relate the biblical account and understand what it literally says—that our

67. Ibid., 104; Campbell, *Preaching Jesus*, 191.

68. Campbell, *Preaching Jesus*, 193.

preaching be an act of telling those stories to others."[69] The telling of the story in preaching is not simply an exercise in communicating information. It is necessary to "relate the story in the same dynamic, compelling literary style found in Scripture itself . . ."[70] It is by telling the biblical stories that listeners come to know God and Jesus Christ.

As we have just seen, it is Ellingsen's contention that a narrative text demands to be read literally. Associated with this position is a rejection of what he refers to as "allegorical" approaches to the Scriptures.[71] An allegorical approach is one that relies on a correlation of Christian symbols and human experience. A well-known example of this is the attempt to correlate the kerygma with existentialist philosophy (as, for example, in the work of Bultmann and Tillich). Ellingsen rejects the correlational approach because in his opinion it imposes extrabiblical categories on the biblical narratives. For his part, he chooses the Reformation teaching of *sola scriptura* (or at least one important aspect of it). Ellingsen states that he is informed by the principle that Scripture is used to interpret Scripture.

Ellingsen rejects all preaching strategies that introduce alien concepts and categories into the biblical narratives. In this context, he avers that to tell a secular story featuring a "Christ figure" is to describe a character other than Jesus.[72] However, he also states that a commitment to a descriptive, literalistic interpretation does not preclude reading Old Testament and New Testament miracle stories from the perspective of Christ's death and resurrection. "We can only discern continuity in the Bible," he contends, "if its entire content points to Christ, particularly his cross and resurrection . . . To interpret the Old Testament and the New Testament miracle accounts as figures is to say that they are fulfilled, properly understood, in relation to Jesus Christ."[73]

What the preacher is essentially aiming to do, according to Ellingsen, is to render the world of the Bible—a world that is constructed around the speech and acts of God in Christ—for her listeners. Following Erich Auerbach's view of the biblical stories, he contends that they assert a "tyrannical" authority. That is, the Bible claims an exclusive authority; it demands that we

---

69. Ellingsen, *Integrity of Biblical Narrative*, 28.

70. Ibid., 38.

71. Ibid., 19–20, 27, 46.

72. Ibid., 79.

73. Ibid.

adjust our personal stories to fit the story it tells.[74] If the stories are told in the right manner, the listeners will become acutely aware of the need to align their attitudes, values, and actions with those of the main characters:

> Yahweh's address to the people of Israel is also God's Word to us today. We, as characters in that account, have an identity—the identity of one who has died to sin in baptism and so no longer can live in it (Rom. 6: 1–4). Similarly, we may respond to cultural dynamics that demand we adapt to radical changes the future is bringing, with St. Paul's words: "Therefore, if anyone is in Christ, he is a new creation; the old has passed away, behold the new has come" (1 Cor. 5:17). We are the Corinthians to whom has been entrusted the message of God reconciling himself to the world through the making of all things new.

Though there are obviously a number of important facets in Ellingsen's approach, the one that stands out in the context of the kind of the work I am doing in this book—apart from the obvious fact that he places God in Christ at the center of the sermon—is his stern opposition to a correlational approach. In the next section, attention is given to this issue.

God At the Center of the Therapeutic Sermon: Correlating Divine and Human Therapy

Therapeutic preaching, as I understand it, is essentially bringing the divine *therapeia* in the Scriptures to bear on the intrapsychic, interpersonal, and developmental challenges that people commonly face. While practical theologians may generally support this type of preaching when it is defined in this way, virtually all offer strong criticism of the psychologized approach that is all too common today.[75] Sadly, there are those preachers who

74. Ibid., 36.

75. The following critiques of psychologized preaching are typical of what one finds in the literature. Lee Ramsey has this to say: "Pastoral care has tended to hog the pulpit over the past thirty to forty years in mainstream Protestantism. Preachers have noticed that the sounds coming from many pulpits have often been the psychological tones of therapeutic preaching. In the name of pastoral concern for the hearer, the preacher has often shrunk the grand and awesome mystery of God-with-us down to the miniature size of the individual psyche" (*Care-full Preaching*, 3). Kay Northcutt makes a similar point: "Preaching [that treats congregants like clients] becomes a therapeutic message to a group of hurting individuals in a hurting world rather than a formational message toward shaping the body of Christ that we are to become. Pastors and congregants take their eyes off the work of God that is ours to do in the world" (*Kindling Desire*, 48).

in the course of attempting to help their listeners cope with the stresses, distresses, and pain of life, point first and foremost not to God's grace in Christ but rather to psychology and insights from the counseling theorists. Human problems and human wisdom in dealing with those problems are set up as the central frame of reference for preaching. In the more crass forms of therapeutic preaching, what is offered is little more than a diluted dose of the therapist's medicine.

The form of therapeutic preaching that is advocated in this book is one that names the divine *therapeia*. The preacher takes her lead primarily from the message of God's therapy that is found in the particular text she is working with. Depending on the text, the note that is sounded will be one of comfort, or forgiveness, or acceptance, or challenge—or a combination of these. God in Christ is very much at the center in this form of therapeutic preaching.

I expect that those whose theological commitments align with one or more of the approaches outlined above will at this point be saying, "Three cheers!" Despite their different emphases and disagreements (some of which are substantial), the proponents of neo-orthodoxy, the new herme-neutic, and postliberalism agree in terms of a fundamental definition of preaching. Preaching for all of them is essentially a liturgical naming of the grace of God in Christ. One very significant point on which they differ is on the use of perspectives from contemporary cultural sources in the sermon. Those in the Barthian school, and the two postliberal theologians we sur-veyed, rule out any attempt to integrate relevant psychological, philosophi-cal, or sociological insights with the gospel message. In commenting on the way in which some theologians (especially Bultmann and Tillich) employ existentialist categories to interpret the message of Christ, Hans Frei gets to the nub of the concern. Frei notes first that correlational theologians bring the categories of human self-alienation or self-distortion on the one hand, and authentic existence on the other, to bear on the identity of Jesus. He then proceeds to point up what he sees as the major flaw in this approach, along with his proposal for a more helpful one:

> But . . . have not the "formal" categories for identification really taken over the person and the story in this analysis? Have not Jesus and his story been forced into a preconceived pattern—whether the right or wrong one? We conclude that, instead of this, the proper procedure is first to look at the story, under as few catego-ries and as formal a scheme of categories for identity description as possible, to see what it tells us about Jesus' identity . . .[76]

76. Frei, *Identity of Jesus*, 101.

Those who take the Barthian view or the narrative perspective we have discussed contend that in naming the grace of God in Christ in a sermon, the preacher should simply follow the line of the story that the text is telling. That is, the role of the preacher is to let the message, with all its power, unfold in the presence of the congregation. The story is approached on its own terms, in its own frame of reference; alien elements should not be imported in. The danger in correlation, so the argument goes, is that the perspective of existentialist philosophy or of psychotherapeutic psychology will distort the biblical one. If a particular culture-shaped soundtrack is playing in the background whenever a preacher comes to a text, it is likely that the Gospel music will be drowned out. That is, the text is not allowed to keep its own shape; it gets forced into the preconceived pattern of the psychological or philosophical school that the preacher is working with.

When I stated that therapeutic preaching needs to put God in Christ firmly at the center, I heard everybody barracking. But in making my next move, I will inevitably lose half my cheer squad. That move is this: I contend that in naming the divine *therapeia* in a sermon, it is particularly helpful to include a correlation with relevant counseling theory. It is acknowledged that the threat of forcing the divine therapy into a psychotherapeutic mold is real. The preacher who follows my approach is advised to bring her store of counseling knowledge with her to her engagement with the text. If she is undisciplined, or lacking in insight, she may well end up twisting the biblical story to fit her preconceived therapeutic pattern. There is certainly a significant risk involved here, but I contend that it is one well worth taking. Those who advocate a correlational approach to preaching, biblical interpretation, and theology do so because they believe that the potential for a rich yield is high. That is, the underlying conviction is that the psychological or philosophical concepts that are brought to biblical and theological study shed their own unique and penetrating light. They produce valuable insights and perspectives that are not otherwise available. In the end, it is a matter of judgment as to whether a particular piece of correlational work distorts or enlightens theology, Bible study, or preaching. In the next chapter, we will discuss the correlational approach to preaching in much greater detail.

4

Connecting Two Worlds

The Case for Correlation

A CENTRAL FEATURE OF the model of therapeutic preaching that I am proposing is the use of psychotherapeutic psychology to draw out important aspects of the divine *therapeia* in the text that is the focus of the sermon. In this way, a correlation is effected between divine and human therapy. The argument being put is that engagement with relevant psychology allows both the preacher and the congregation to see something in the text that would otherwise have been missed. Not everyone, needless to say, is happy with this approach. Some will object (I have particularly in mind those who take a Barthian or narrative approach to preaching) that this procedure involves the introduction of an alien element into the sermon. They contend that the text should simply be allowed to speak on its own terms; it is neither necessary nor helpful to call upon a non-theological discipline to aid in its explication. Against this view, I will argue that a judicious use of the correlational method is quite possible. In this approach, the preacher does not distort the meaning of the text but rather draws out an aspect of it in a way that is genuinely helpful.

Rather than carrying out a discussion of the method of correlation in the abstract, I will proceed by working with concrete examples. In order to set the scene for the debate over this issue, three famous and influential cases of correlational theology will be presented: Friedrich Schleiermacher's "feeling of absolute dependence," Paul Tillich's "New Being," and Karl Rahner's "anonymous faith." When we are discussing below the strengths and dangers in the method, reference will be made to these approaches.

We will begin our discussion with the approach sponsored by the father of modern Protestant theology.

Schleiermacher: The Feeling of Absolute Dependence

Paul Tillich refers to Schleiermacher's approach to religion (as he does to his own) as an apologetic or "answering theology."[1] Schleiermacher attempted to provide cogent and compelling answers to the pressing intellectual questions of his time. The latter part of the eighteenth century was a time when theology was confronted with the imposing challenges posed by critical historical research, scientific explanation of the natural world, confusion and doubt over, and, in some quarters, downright rejection of religious authority, acute awareness of religious pluralism and the implications for belief in special revelation. The most urgent and difficult question, however, that confronted the theologian in this epoch was how to communicate a meaningful concept of God in a cultural context in which immediate experience and empirical observation were widely held to be the only reliable tools for building the knowledge and directing the action of humanity. Schleiermacher responded to this challenge by positing the "feeling of absolute dependence" as the essence of religion and the fundamental form of the human's relation to God. Immediate awareness or "intuition" is identified as the central dynamic in religious experience.

Though the notes sounded loudest in his novel theological approach are those of Romanticism, Schleiermacher does not reject the Enlightenment outright. Indeed, some of his ideas are linked to the thought of that towering figure of the Enlightenment, Immanuel Kant. The Enlightenment thinkers championed autonomy, reason, and freedom in the face of what they saw as the oppressive forces of religious and social tradition, the authoritarian rule of monarchs, and the darkness of superstition. An individual should not blindly follow the direction of figures of authority in determining her view of personal, social, political, and religious life; rather, she should apply her autonomous reason to this task.

Kant took the same line as all of the Enlightenment thinkers in that he identified reason as the key to human knowledge; however he proposed a fundamental shift in the approach to the scope and role of rational thought. He averred that human reason can only deal with the sensible empirical world. The "phenomena" perceived by the senses are interpreted by the

1. Tillich, *History of Christian Thought*, 391.

innate or *a priori* categories of the mind. Thus, "unity," "plurality," and "causality" are not entities that form part of the essential structure of the world but rather are categories by which the mind organizes its perceptions into a coherent pattern. That is to say, human knowledge is a synthetic creation of the mind achieved through the operation of innate mental categories applied to external data.

Traditional metaphysical systems used in theology and proofs of God's existence were dismissed by Kant. He contended that human reason can only be legitimately applied to the spatio-temporal world. Kant's aim, though, was not to destroy faith. Instead, he argued for a new approach to it: the real basis of faith is found in the human's moral experience, in "practical" rather than in "pure" reason. According to Kant, humans possess an awareness of a "categorical imperative," an innate sense of moral duty. The fact that human beings follow the dictates of the categorical imperative points to the existence of a moral law-giver. That is, the existence of God is implied by the moral sense that all humans are endowed with.

Romanticism was a reaction against the Enlightenment. The movement reached its peak in the early part of the nineteenth century. It is notoriously difficult to capture the essence of Romanticism. For our purposes, it suffices to say that it is a cultural ethos grounded in a celebration of nature rather than civilization, in deep appreciation for, and valuation of, art and creativity, and in a valuing of intuition and emotions over reason and the intellect.[2] Given that art and human creativity were central concerns for those in the Romantic movement, it is natural that they looked at the world in terms of aesthetic categories. Here Kant's thought made a valuable contribution through his *Critique of Judgment*. In his early work, he provided a theoretical basis for a scientific analysis of both the natural world (*Critique of Pure Reason*) and the moral imperative (*Critique of Practical Reason*). In his third critique, *Critique of Judgment*, Kant found a principle of unity for pure and practical reason. Paul Tillich captures this link well:

> The moral always commands while the theoretical analyses. Is there a union between them? . . . Is there something in nature which, so to speak, fulfills the commands of the moral imperative

---

2. Helpful discussions of Romanticism are provided in Tillich, *History of Christian Thought*, 372–86; Crouter, in his introduction to Schleiermacher, *On Religion*, 18–39; and Clements, *Friedrich Schleiermacher*, 12–15.

and transcends the mere scientific analysis of nature? [Kant] discovered . . . the organic in nature and the aesthetic in culture.[3]

It is to be expected, then, that adherents to the Romantic ideal would be attracted to the *Critique of Judgment*. Romantic philosophy viewed aesthetic intuition as the impulse driving the religious sensibility. Indeed, art is religion itself. At the center of Schleiermacher's *On Religion* (1799) is the notion of an aesthetic intuition of the universe.

In his attempts to provide theological answers to the questions thrown up by his contemporaries, Schleiermacher drew on both Kant and Romanticism. Indeed, Schleiermacher's engagement with Kant led him into the counter-Enlightenment movement. Richard Crouter observes that: "The critical encounter with Kant's moral and religious philosophy served as a bridge to his involvement in the romantic movement. The clash that raged over the status of moral-rational or aesthetic-intuitional categories in shaping our basic views of the world preoccupied his early years and laid the groundwork for his subsequent development."[4]

If the aesthetic element in human experience was a significant influence from Romanticism on Schleiermacher's theology, the identity principle was clearly the most important.[5] According to this principle, every human experience is at the same time an experience of the infinite. The Infinite Life expresses itself through the processes of both the natural world and human history. This could be construed as pantheism. However, the term should not be taken to indicate that God is everything. The principle of identity should not be construed as suggesting that God is literally this tree, this horse, and so on, but rather that the world has an absolute ground of unity in God.

The way in which Schleiermacher interprets religion is shaped very significantly by the fundamental assumptions and principles postulated by both the Enlightenment and Romanticism. But this does not mean that he thought that the important thinkers in these movements had the last word to say on all matters to do with religion and human existence. He did take on board the view that the human person is at the center of critical thought

---

3. Tillich, *History of Christian Thought*, 379.

4. Crouter, in his introduction to Schleiermacher, *On Religion*, 19.

5. On the central role of the identity principle in Schleiermacher's theology, see Tillich, *History of Christian Thought*, 372–74, 390–391; Clements, *Friedrich Schleiermacher*, 12–13; Crouter, his introduction to Schleiermacher, *On Religion*, 38; and Immink, *Faith*, 38

and practical living. In line with this, he accepted the critique that says that the way in which God is articulated in orthodox Christian theology makes God a threat and limit to human freedom. So in line with the leading intellectuals of his epoch, Schleiermacher identified the quest to understand what it is to be truly and fully human as being of vital importance. However, he contended that philosophers, poets, and artists of his time had not taken us to the heart of human existence. The religious experience takes an individual and a community into the essence of what it is to be human. According to Schleiermacher, God should not be thought of as the Supreme Being who sits outside the world and controls and limits humans. Rather, God is the unifying ground of all human experience. Every act of human self-consciousness is at the same time an experience of God.

In his early work *On Religion*, Schleiermacher states this intention: "I wish to lead you into the innermost depths from which religion first addresses the mind. I wish to show you from what capacity of humanity religion proceeds, and how it belongs to what is for you the highest and dearest."[6] In this apologetical work, Schleiermacher argues that the human capacity at the heart of religious experience is not knowing (metaphysics) or doing (morality) but "intuition of the universe." Metaphysics and morality include in their purview only human activity, but religion seeks to experience the infinite, to become aware of its "imprint and manifestation."[7] Though "speculation" and "praxis" have a role to play in religion, its essence is found in intuition and feeling. When Schleiermacher refers to intuition of the universe he means immediate awareness. Here is the core of religious experience. To encounter the natural world in self-consciousness is at the same time to encounter God. This is the identity principle referred to above: any experience of the finite is at once an experience of the infinite. In a sensory intuition of an object in the world,

> [a] manifestation, an event develops quickly and magically into an image of the universe. Even as the beloved and ever-sought-for form fashions itself, my soul flees toward it. I embrace it, not as a shadow, but as the holy essence itself. I lie on the bosom of the infinite world. At this moment I am its soul, for I feel all its powers and its infinite life as my own; at this moment it is my body, for I penetrate its

6. Schleiermacher, *On Religion*, 87.

7. Ibid., 104.

muscles and its limbs as my own, and its innermost nerves move according to my sense and my presentiment as my own.[8]

In his mature thought, Schleiermacher retains the trinity of religious experience—knowing, doing, and self-consciousness—however the essence is now seen not simply to be intuition of the universe but rather the "feeling of absolute dependence." It is important to note that he does not use the word "feeling" in the sense of a psychological state—a natural interpretation for those of us participating in a therapeutic culture. What is meant is rather immediate awareness or self-awareness. In every instance of self-consciousness there are two factors in play: that which is "self-caused" and that which is "non-self-caused."[9] This observation relates to the fact that the awareness of the ego is always awareness of something. The senses and the mind are directed to a particular object outside the self. Thus, the two poles of self-consciousness are "receptivity" and "activity." It is the former dynamic that is associated with the feeling of dependence: self-consciousness is simply impossible in the absence of an Other. Activity, on the one hand, is associated with a feeling of freedom. In relation to the finite world (nature), there is never a state of absolute dependency. This is so because along with the experience of receptivity, there is also in every case an experience of activity. An individual receives sense impressions, but she also acts on the object that is associated with those impressions. That is, in any relation with an object in the world, there is always an element of freedom. Yet in the very experience of receptivity and activity, an individual is immediately conscious of the fact that her experience is grounded in a source outside herself. Thus, the feeling of absolute dependence is also a relation to God. Schleiermacher puts it this way: "The *Whence* of our receptive and active existence, as implied in this self-consciousness, is to be designated by the word 'God,' and . . . this is for us the really original signification of that word."[10] "God-consciousness" is the term around which Schleiermacher builds his whole systematic theology. It is at the center of his interpretation of every major Christian doctrine.

8. Ibid., 113.

9. Schleiermacher, *Christian Faith*, para 4, sect. 1.

10. Ibid., para. 4, sect. 4.

Tillich and the New Being

A fundamental requirement of legitimate correlational work is the maintenance of both autonomy and reciprocity in the relations between Christian
theology and modern learning. Schleiermacher was keenly aware of this. In
a letter to his friend Lücke, he had this to say:

> If the reformation in which our church has its origins has not
> the objective to establish a perpetual alliance between the living
> Christian faith and that scientific research which is in every re-
> spect free to explore and to pursue its own ends independently,
> so that faith does not hinder learning, nor learning exclude faith,
> then that reformation is not adequate for the needs of our time
> and we require yet another one, regardless of the extent of struggle
> required to bring it about. But it is my firm conviction that the
> basis for this alliance was already established earlier in that first
> reformation . . .[11]

Tillich has something quite similar to say; he describes his correlational approach as "a unity of the dependence and independence of two
factors."[12] The "two factors" are the "eternal message" of the Christian faith
and an existentialist interpretation of being. Tillich seeks to use the answers
supplied by revealed theology to respond to the questions raised by the
interpretation of human existence provided by philosophy, psychology,
drama, art, literature, and poetry.

The first major condition for a valid correlation of the Christian heritage and cultural self-interpretation is maintenance of the independence
of each domain. According to Tillich, the existential question—the human
person engaged with the struggles and conflicts in her existence—is not
the source for the answers that theology provides. "[Humankind] is the
question, not the answer."[13] It is also wrong to draw the question of human
existence out of the eternal message. The revelatory answer is meaningless,
suggest Tillich, if it is not tied into questions that contemporary people are
asking.

Correlation also obviously requires mutual dependence in the relations between the two partners. Herein lies a fundamental danger. Tillich is acutely aware of this. He refers to the "difficult problem" of mutual

11. Schleiermacher, *Schleiermacher-Auswahl* cited in Clayton, *Concept of Correlation*,
40.

12. Tillich, *Systematic Theology II*, 13. Hereafter referred to as *ST II*.

13. Ibid.

dependence in correlational work. He refers to the traps associated with it in these terms: "Since Schleiermacher, it [i.e., the problem of mutual dependence] has also been present whenever a philosophy of religion was used as an entering door into the theological system, and the problem arose of how far the door determines the structure of the house, or the house the door."[14] Put differently, one potential pitfall is an improper application of cultural self-interpretation resulting in a twisting of the Christian symbols out of shape; the other is that the cultural self-interpretation is distorted to serve the needs of theological interpretation. Tillich indicates how he intends to guard against these dangers (although he recognizes that no methodological principle is fail-safe). In order to protect the integrity of the eternal message, first, it is necessary for the mediating theologian to base all of her work on the foundation of Jesus as the Christ.[15] The second safeguard is a commitment by the theologian to fully experience the challenges associated with the human condition while acting as if she has to do it without the benefit of the resources of faith:

> [The theologian] must participate in [humankind's] finitude, which is also [her] own, and in its anxiety as though [she] had never received the revelatory answer of "eternity." [She] must participate in [humankind's] estrangement, which is also [her] own, and show the anxiety of guilt as though [she] had never received the revelatory answer of "forgiveness." The theologian does not rest on the theological answer that [she] announces. [She] can give it in a convincing way only if [she] participates with [her] whole being in the situation of the question, namely, the human predicament.[16]

Tillich's basic intent is to engage with existentialist thought, while always respecting its autonomy. In referring to the research of the existentialists, he observes that a central feature of it is the recognition of the gap between existence and essence, between being-in-the-world and true being. The existence of the individual is characterized by an underlying anxiety and sense of meaninglessness. Tillich avers that existentialism has very effectively analyzed the "old eon"—the era in which life is lived in estrangement. Thus, the human is the question that theology must provide a compelling answer to. Since existentialism provides such a comprehensive

14. Ibid., 14.

15. Tillich, *Systematic Theology I*, 64. Hereafter referred to as *ST I*.

16. Tillich, *ST II*, 15.

and insightful analysis of the human situation, Tillich refers to it as "the good luck" of Christian theology:

> It has helped to rediscover the classical Christian interpretation of human existence. Any theological attempt to do this would not have had the same effect. This positive use refers not only to existentialist philosophy but also to analytic psychology, literature, poetry, drama, and art. In all these realms there is an immense amount of material which the theologian can use and organize in an attempt to present Christ as the answer to the questions implied within existence.[17]

In essence, then, the task of theology in Tillich's view is to supply the answers provided by revelation to the questions raised by creative cultural self-interpretation. Ultimately, theology only has one answer. "God," says Tillich, "is the answer to the question implied in being."[18] Tillich's approach to the question of God is to develop its various elements using the language and concepts of existentialist ontology. He uses four ontological "categories" or "structures of finite being and thinking"[19] and three ontological "elements" to shape his interpretation of the question of God. The four categories are time, space, causality, and substance.[20] It should be noted that there are other ontological categories—e.g., quality and quantity—but these are excluded by Tillich since they are not theologically relevant. The three elements are individualization and participation, dynamics and form, and freedom and destiny. We will discuss the categories first.

The ontological categories are the forms through which the mind engages with the world. That is, they are the innate cognitive structures identified by Kant that determine the form of the human encounter with reality. Tillich suggests that the four categories he has signified as theologically relevant all express both the union of being and non-being, and the union of anxiety and courage.[21] In this statement, we find identified four of the really significant existentialist concepts. Non-being, first, plays a vital role in existentialist ontology. Tillich observes that the human knows that she lacks the "aseity" attributed to God. She is not the ground of her own

17. Ibid., 27.

18. Ibid., 163.

19. Tillich, *ST I*, 165.

20. Ibid.

21. Ibid., 193.

being; she knows herself to be a contingent rather than a necessary being. She therefore lives always under the threat of non-being. It is with this in mind that Heidegger analyzed the meaning of "annihilating nothingness." The human lives in the shadow of the inescapable reality that is death. Sartre includes in non-being not only the threat of nothingness but also the specter of meaninglessness. Tillich avers that existentialist analyzes such as these show that "[the human's] finitude, or creatureliness, is unintelligible without the concept of dialectical nonbeing."[22] Associated with the ever-present possibility of non-being is a deep, underlying anxiety. It is not possible to cure oneself of this anxiety. Existential *angst* is different from psychological fear. Fear can be dealt with through some form of action. But there is no action that can remove the threat of non-being. The human therefore needs the "courage to be." That is, she needs the courage to accept the anxiety that cannot be eliminated.

As indicated above, the theologian offers God as the answer to these existential questions. Tillich conceives of God as being-itself, as the ground of being. Since God is the power which determines the structure of being, God is not subject to the threat of nothingness. To say that God is the power of being is to say also that God is the power to conquer non-being.[23] It also means that God is the condition of the possibility of the human courage to be.

In his approach to the question of God, Tillich also employs the ontological elements mentioned above. The first of these is individualization and participation.[24] It is inherent in the nature of being that it expresses itself in individual entities. This particular person, animal, or tree has certain characteristics which set it apart from the other members sharing its form of being. But it is also in the nature of being that individual entities participate in the larger reality in which they find themselves. An animal participates in its environment, and a human person participates in her world. The human participates in the universe through the rational structures that exist in the mind and in reality. The other essential form of participation is, of course, interpersonal communion.

The second ontological element that Tillich develops in order to apply it to the question of God is dynamics and form. To be something means to

22. Ibid., 189.

23. Tillich, *ST II*, 11.

24. Tillich, *ST I*, 175–78.

have a form. Form is that which makes a thing what it is. It is its "definite power of being."[25] The form of a tree is what makes it a tree; it is that which makes it an expression of treehood.

Dynamics is a dialectical concept. It refers to the potentiality of being. A thing is imbued with power to actualize its potential. A child, for example, is endowed with certain physical, intellectual, psychological, and spiritual potentialities. These are (partially) actualized over time. But as she grows and matures, the transcendence of previous states never results in a loss of her essential nature, of her humanness. That is, self-transcendence exists in a dialectical relationship with self-conservation.

The dynamic nature of human being is also expressed in what Tillich refers to as vitality. While the dynamics of subhuman life are subject to the limits of natural necessity, in human life the dynamic element is open in all directions. The human has the power to "create a world beyond the given world."[26]

The final element in Tillich's system is freedom and destiny.[27] Animals are fully determined by natural instincts. Humans are also under the sway of certain basic drives, but they are not completely controlled by them; they have the capacity to partially transcend nature. Freedom is expressed in the power of deliberation, decision, and responsibility.

The human, however, is not completely free. The decisions she makes, and the actions she takes, are set within a total context that is constituted by factors such as body structure, personality type, intellect, spirituality, and familial and cultural background. This complex of factors is what Tillich means by destiny. Destiny is "myself as given, formed by nature, history, and myself. My destiny is the basis of my freedom; my freedom participates in shaping my destiny."[28]

Together the categories and elements provide a description of the ontological structure of being. It is this structure which Tillich says supplies the material for an interpretation of the divine life.[29] In this way, he effects a correlation between the ontological structure and the revealed nature of God. The word "revealed" is important here. Tillich is very clear that he is

25. Ibid., 178.

26. Ibid., 180.

27. Ibid., 182–86.

28. Ibid., 185.

29. Ibid., 243.

not implying that a doctrine of God can be derived from an ontological system. The essential source of our knowledge of the character of God is revelation: "Theology can only explain and systematize the existential knowledge of revelation in theoretical terms, interpreting the symbolic significance of the ontological elements and categories."[30]

According to Tillich, the only non-symbolic statement we can make about God is that God is the ground or power of being. The statement "God is being-itself" means what it says "directly and properly."[31] To speak of God as living, creating, and related is to engage in symbolic language. The ontological terms and concepts that Tillich develops are used to interpret these symbols for God. In this way, he attempts an "existential correlation of [humanity] and God."[32] The terms that are used to describe the essential nature of human existence—space, time, causality, individualization and participation, freedom and destiny, etc.—are also used in the interpretation of the symbols for God.

We note in passing, therefore, that he employs the *analogia entis* (analogy of being) that also features in the correlational model I propose for therapeutic preaching. Barth, on the other hand, stresses the infinite qualitative distinction between time and eternity. What this means is that analogical use of ontological terms to aid in the interpretation of what has been revealed about God in and through the Word obscures rather than enlightens. Human ontological categories are so vastly different to divine ones that their theological employment is inevitably misleading and distorting. There is much more that could be said here; we will hold that for the next chapter.

I indicated above that estrangement is identified by existentialists as a fundamental factor in the experience of being-in-the-world. The human as she exists is not what she essentially is. That is, the tragic situation of the human is that she must live with a gap between her essence and her existence. She lives estranged from her true being. Though estrangement is not a biblical term, Tillich contends that many of the scriptural descriptions of the human predicament point in its direction:

> It is implied in the symbols of the expulsion from paradise, in the hostility between [humanity] and nature, in the deadly hostility of

30. Ibid., 243.

31. Ibid., 238.

32. Ibid., 248.

brother against brother, in the estrangement of nation from nation through the confusion of language, and in the continuous complaints of the prophets against their kings and people who turn to alien gods. Estrangement is implied in Paul's statement that man perverted the image of God into that of idols, in his classical description of "[the human] against himself," in his vision of [human] hostility against [other humans] as combined with his distorted desires.[33]

A major aim of Tillich's is a correlation of sin and estrangement. He begins by suggesting that the experience of estrangement is not identical to that of sin.[34] Sin is essentially a state of estrangement from God, one's self, and one's world. Nevertheless, sin has its own unique meaning; it is sharply expressive of personal freedom and guilt in a way that estrangement is not. This is not to say, says Tillich, that there is no personal element associated with estrangement. It is simply the case that the personal dimension is at the forefront in sin in a way that it is not in estrangement. The nature of the correlation is expressed by Tillich in this way: "Sin is a universal fact before it becomes an individual act, or more precisely, sin as an individual act actualizes the universal fact of estrangement."[35]

Tillich identifies unbelief, concupiscence, and *hubris* as the three "marks" of human estrangement.[36] Unbelief, first, is that act in which a person turns away from God with the whole of her being. In her way-of-being-in-the-world, she turns toward herself and her world and thereby breaks the essential unity with the ground of her being.

Hubris, second, is for Tillich fundamentally self-elevation and self-affirmation. The essential nature of the human being is to belong to God. Estrangement is the denial of this belongingness. The dignity and greatness of the human are found in her self-consciousness or total centeredness. In her self-consciousness, the human has the ability to transcend both herself and her world. The downside of the human's greatness is the temptation to make herself the center of her existence and of her world. In an act of self-elevation, the human reaches out for the infinite. *Hubris* is essentially "the hidden desire to be like God."[37]

33. Tillich, *ST II*, 45.
34. Ibid., 46.
35. Ibid., 56.
36. Ibid., 47.
37. Ibid., 51.

Concupiscence, lastly, is defined by Tillich as the manifestation of a desire to draw everything in one's world into oneself. The desire for knowledge, sex, and power is a good within prescribed limits. Concupiscence is expressed in the unlimited character of the striving for these things.

Some of this thinking is expressed in Tillich's famous sermon, "You are Accepted."[38] He opines that both the word "sin" and the word "grace" are strange to the modern mind. They are strange because they are so well known. He suggests to his listeners that they might like to try another word in order to grasp the meaning behind sin. It is of course "estrangement." However, he uses a more familiar word to ease his auditors into the concept. That word is "separation." The human person experiences separation from others, from herself, and from the Ground of Being. Grace overcomes the separation and estrangement that we all experience. Grace reunites that which has been separated. The message of hope that Tillich offers to his listeners is this: "Grace is the *reunion* of life with life, the *reconciliation* of the self with itself. Grace is the acceptance of that which is rejected."[39] The strange word "grace" is translated by the familiar one—"acceptance." The voice of healing says:

> You are accepted. *You are accepted*, accepted by that which is greater than you, and the name of which you do not know. Do not ask for the name now; perhaps you will find it later. Do not try to do anything now; perhaps later you will do much. Do not seek for anything; do not perform anything; do not intend anything. *Simply accept the fact that you are accepted!*[40]

It is noteworthy that Tillich uses a central term from psychotherapy in his attempt to renew the power of the word "grace" for his listeners. When Tillich fled from the Nazi regime in Germany and settled in the United States, he joined the New York Psychology Group. Here he engaged with some very influential theologians and psychotherapists—men such as Seward Hiltner, Erich Fromm, Carl Rogers, and Rollo May.[41] The exchanges he had with these men opened a new vista for him in relation to his correlational method. He recognized that psychotherapeutic insights into the mental and spiritual malaise that many modern people experience can be linked to traditional

38. Tillich, *Shaking of the Foundations*.

39. Ibid., 158.

40. Ibid., 163 (emphasis in the original).

41. On the impact of the New York Psychology Group on Tillich, see Graham et al, *Theological Reflection*, 155.

symbols of the faith. That is, concepts such as guilt, repression, and acceptance can be correlated with sin, grace, and forgiveness.

It is important to recognize, however, that Tillich did not believe that the traditional theological terms can simply be replaced with psycho-therapeutic correlates. "Sin" and "grace" have their own unique, irreducible meanings and connotations. "Separation" and "acceptance" capture the essence of the faith symbols, but these contemporary concepts do not exhaust the meaning of the traditional ones.

The meaning of "Jesus the Christ" is developed in this correlational frame. Christ is the power of grace—the One who overcomes estrangement. The anxiety, guilt, meaninglessness, and despair identified by the existentialists as the marks of estrangement are construed by Tillich as the marks of the old eon. Christ is the one who ushers in a new eon. Tillich interprets Christ as enacting the replacement of the Old Being with the New Being.

Tillich suggests that when Paul talks about becoming a new creation in Christ, we should interpret this as participation in the newness of being which is in Christ. Christ is the bearer of the New Being. "The term 'New Being' . . . points directly to the cleavage between essential and existential being . . . The New Being is new in so far as it is the undistorted manifestation of essential being within the conditions of existence."[42] In a word, to become a new creation in Christ means to be restored to one's true being. Clearly, this can only be restoration in principle. The gap between essence and existence will continue in actuality until the New Being is manifested in all its fullness in the eschaton.

Rahner and Faith As Courage

Karl Rahner is famous for his concept of "anonymous faith." Like Tillich, he uses existentialist philosophy as a conversation partner. Rahner achieves his fresh approach to faith through a correlation of Thomist theology with existentialist thought in general and with the thought of Martin Heidegger in particular. He provides us with a number of examples of what anonymous Christianity means in practice; here one very important case is presented—namely, faith as courage. As we shall see, Rahner picks up on the crucial existential challenge of affirming one's existence in the face of the threat of non-being (Tillich's "courage to be").

42. Tillich, *ST II*, 119.

Rahner defines anonymous faith as faith that is necessary and effective for salvation but which occurs without an explicit and conscious relationship to the revelation of Jesus Christ.[43] It is an extension of his concept of the "supernatural existential." Because there is this factor in human existence, there is no dualism between nature and grace. Humans do not operate according to two distinct drives—one toward purely natural fulfillment and the other toward the vision of God. Rather, human existence is graced existence. We have a capacity to receive God's loving gift of God's self. "This 'existential' is a permanent modification of the human spirit which transforms its natural dynamism into an ontological drive to the God of grace and glory."[44] The fact of the supernatural existential means that there is no aspect of human action in which God's grace is not communicated. Thus, whenever a person acts in good conscience, she is experiencing—albeit implicitly—God's grace.

According to Rahner, the human person is the being who has the capacity for unlimited transcendence in knowledge and freedom. In our human experience, we are oriented to God. This transcendent reference of the human is mediated through what Rahner calls "categorial" reality— the concrete, everyday stuff of life. The aspects of this categorial reality are not necessarily religious in nature. Thus, whenever a person faces up to moral decisions honestly and courageously, she accepts herself in her self-transcending subjectivity, and thereby accepts God.

The grace that is God's self-communication—received in the act of absolute fidelity to conscience—transforms human consciousness. When God gives God's self to a person, that person comes to a conscious, though non-thematic, knowledge of her unlimited transcendence. That is, through God's gracious action there is awareness of the radical nature of the transcendent element in human existence, but it is only a tacit awareness. Rahner puts it this way:

> The process by which human transcendence is given new depth and purpose and is ordered to the direct presence of God is universal in time and place, because God's saving will is universally operative, even if it cannot be distinguished or given conceptual shape by individual reflection. If God's self-communication is free and if it is consciously grasped by a person, even if this occurs

---

43. See Rahner, "Anonymous and Explicit Faith," 52–59.

44. McCool, in his introduction to "Relationship between Nature and Grace," 185.

without thematic reflection, then the . . . conditions for supernatural revelation are realized . . .[45]

Rahner's teaching on "faith as courage"[46] represents an explicit working out of his general theory of anonymous faith. As the phrase itself indicates, his aim is to achieve a correlation between the existential factor
(courage) and the theological virtue (faith). Rahner begins his discussion
on faith and courage by observing that courage is really the same thing as
hope. And he sees hope as ultimately hope for God.

Courage, says Rahner, is necessary when there is a risk involved in a
certain action or process. Risk comes into play when there is no guaran-
tee of success. This occurs when there is a gap between what, on the one
hand, a person plans for and hopes will happen, and what, on the other
hand, might in fact happen. Rahner states that "courage certainly can, even
should, co-exist with planning, with working out the chances of success.
But where courage is really required is when there is a gap for rational
consideration between the calculation of the possibilities of success and
the actual performance of the task, where success is not known for certain
before it is actually achieved."[47]

Of course there are activities and processes involving different degrees
of courage. For example, there is certainly a gap between what can be rea-
sonably planned for and controlled and what might actually happen in the
experience of the (not so proficient) home handyperson who embarks on
the task of tiling the bathroom. However, Rahner is speaking about "radical
total" courage. This is courage that involves the whole person. It is the kind
of courage Tillich refers to in *The Courage to Be*.[48] As we have seen, Tillich
speaks of the courage required to affirm one's existence in the face of the
threat of non-being. The whole person, the person in the totality of her existence, is involved in the courage to be. Rahner makes reference to the way
in which the whole person is involved in the courageous act of facing up
to the challenge of self-realization. Self-realization is the human's "first and
last task." In this task, a person is wholly and completely herself in freedom.
However, the fulfillment of this ultimate task depends on a whole host of
conditions and causes that cannot be controlled. There is an experience of
one's freedom as "limited and threatened." Here, then, is the gulf that was

45. Rahner, "Anonymous and Explicit Faith," 57.

46. Rahner, *Freedom and the Spirit*.

47. Ibid., 15.

48. Tillich, *Courage to Be*.

referred to above. The only way that this gulf can be bridged is by absolute hope. This hope Rahner calls revealed faith.

Freedom always involves the taking of a risk. In the experience of risk one comes "face to face with the incomprehensibility and freedom of God."[49] The hope that bridges the gulf is ultimately hope for God. Grace, says Rahner, makes it possible for the human to reach out for the goal of hope—namely God. Here is true revelation, though it need not be consciously understood as such. This is not a revelation involving the communication of a particular dogma; rather, it "springs from the heart and soul of the free person."[50] Thus, grace drives this inner dynamism of hope, making the courage to hope for everything—for God—possible. "This inner spiritual dynamism of [the human] should be accepted and not retarded and reduced by any false modesty . . . so that no other good is sought as the final goal of life. If it is accepted, then what we call faith, in theological terms, is already present."[51]

Correlation Is a Two-Way Street

In general terms, the three theological approaches that we have surveyed are about supplying answers drawn from revealed theology to the questions thrown up by critical cultural reflection. Tillich contrasts this approach with that of what he labels as the "kerygmatic theologians." He sees in these theologians (e.g., Luther and Barth) an emphasis on eternal truth over against the relativities of the human situation.[52] There is an attempt to maintain the power and integrity in the eternal message in the face of the vicissitudes and shifting perspectives in the contemporary culture. While on one level this is laudable, Tillich points out that without a "courageous participation" in the various cultural self-interpretations there is a danger that theology will establish an "exclusive transcendence." Kerygmatic theology must therefore be complemented by an apologetic theology, i.e., an "answering theology." The theologian taking up the apologetic task seeks to answer the questions implied in the situation with the resources of the eternal message. Apologetic theology involves the attempt to step onto the common ground established by the cultural self-interpretations with the intention—emphasized in keryg-

49. Rahner, *Freedom and the Spirit*, 22.

50. Ibid., 22.

51. Ibid., 22–23.

52. Tillich, *ST I*, 4.

matic theology—of grounding all its statements in the eternal message. Its method "tries to correlate the questions implied in the situation with the answers implied in the message."[53] This method of correlation attempts to overcome the potential errors in both the apologetic and kerygmatic approaches to theology. "It does not derive the answers from the questions as a self-defying apologetic theology does. Nor does it elaborate answers without relating them to the questions as a self-defying kerygmatic theology does. It correlates questions and answers, situation and message, human existence and divine manifestation."[54]

The cultural self-interpretation supplies the question; revealed theology supplies the answer. Tillich contends that it is impossible for the existentialists to supply answers because the human is the question. Whenever they do give answers, they do so in either religious or quasi-religious terms.[55] That is, they step out of their role as existentialist philosopher and take on that of religious thinker. In this vein, Pascal drew the material for his answers from the Augustinian tradition, Kierkegaard from the Lutheran, and Marcel from the Thomist. The same applies to the answers offered by the atheistic existentialists. They too are unable to develop answers out of their own questions. The answers of thinkers such as Nietzsche, Sartre, and Heidegger come out of "hidden religious sources."[56]

Tillich is right in his contention that theology cannot afford an "exclusive transcendence" that fails to grapple with the creative self-interpretations generated by culture. He is also correct in insisting that all theological statements addressing cultural expressions need to be grounded in the eternal message (the exact shape of this message is, of course, dependent on the particular interpretive horizon one operates out of). The problem with Tillich's *statement* of theological method—he seems to have carried out his theological reflection differently—is that it does not allow for the possibility that culture may provide real answers to its own questions.

The philosopher of religion, Guyton Hammond, was one of the first to identify this problem.[57] He points out that Tillich overlooks the fact that the estrangement of humankind is only partial. If it was total then it would be true that an existentialist analysis of being would be unable to generate

53. Ibid., 8.

54. Ibid.

55. Tillich, *ST II*, 25–26.

56. Ibid., 26.

57. See Hammond, "Examination of Tillich's Method," 248–51.

any answers. The reality, Hammond argues, is that the humanist thinker is able—to some extent at least—to rise above the experience of alienation, to gain some perspective on it, and to offer some ways to overcome it. That is, she is able to talk meaningfully not only about estrangement but also about reconciliation. She is not so mired in the bog of alienation that she is unable to see how she might set about getting out. Hammond suggests that the way Tillich goes about his work—in contrast to his articulation of his method—seems to constitute an acknowledgement of this. Thus, there is a need for a revised understanding of existentialism. The way in which Hammond frames the matter is close to what would later be referred to as the method of mutual critical correlation:

> [I]deas of both estrangement and reconciliation—the formulation of the "question" as well as the "answer"—are viewed [by Tillich] as religious. Since there is no sharp distinction between question and answer, both are of interest to theology. On the other hand, neither the formulation of the question (estrangement) nor the answer (reconciliation) can be accepted without criticism by theology, for question and answer are interdependent.[58]

Seward Hiltner was also acutely aware of the importance of establishing a genuinely two-way conversation, working as he did to construct a pastoral theology that integrated the truths of the Christian heritage with the insights of the psychotherapeutic tradition. He argued, against Tillich, that a full two-way exchange of commitments is required: "We believe that a full two-way street is necessary in order to describe theological method. If we hold that theology is always assimilation of the faith, not just the abstract idea of the faith apart from its reception, then it becomes necessary to say that culture may find answers to questions raised by culture."[59] Hiltner wanted to find a more adequate term than "correlation" to describe this "two-way street" between faith and culture.[60] The term "dialectic" points to the tension or opposition in the relationship. He was, however, concerned that the connotation of tension it carries may suggest that differences are substantive when often they are only superficial. "Intervolve" has the advantage of communicating the key idea of faith and culture involved with one another; it has the disadvantage, though, of being awkward. The best he could suggest was "amphidetic." An amphidetic inquiry is one that is

58. Ibid., 250.

59. Hiltner, *Preface to Pastoral Theology*, 223.

60. Ibid., 223.

bound all around. While Hiltner's search for a more adequate term seems less than successful, he did grasp the fundamental concept of a mutually critical correlation. He saw that for faith to be relevant it must engage in a "constant and discriminatory dialogue with culture."[61]

David Tracy offers a clear description of the nature of this "discriminatory dialogue." A critical correlative approach will involve "the dramatic confrontation, the mutual illuminations and corrections, the possible basic reconciliation between principal values, cognitive claims, and existential faiths of both a reinterpreted post-modern consciousness and a reinterpreted Christianity."[62] As has been indicated above, there are two principal sources for this correlational work—namely, Christian texts and interpretations of ordinary human experience. It is the task of theology to show the adequacy of the major Christian symbols and themes for describing the totality of human experience.[63] Tracy, like Hammond and Hiltner, shows that Tillich's method does not actually call for a correlation between results from investigations of both cultural interpretations and faith claims.[64] Instead, it asks for a correlation of questions generated by cultural analyses with answers provided in the Christian message. If, Tracy points out, the cultural expressions are taken seriously, their answers to their own questions will be analyzed critically. Christianity claims that its message contains the answers to all questions thrown up by human existence. A critical theology must, therefore, compare the Christian answers with those from all other sources. What is needed, then, is a method capable of correlating the questions and answers from both sources for theological reflection. The questions and answers provided by a reinterpreted Christianity need to be critically correlated with the questions and answers contained in a reinterpreted cultural consciousness.

Ronald Allen builds a model of preaching grounded in the method of mutual critical correlation.[65] He construes the sermon as a conversation in which the partners are the Bible, Christian history, doctrine, and practice, the voices in the wider contemporary Christian community, relevant contributions from philosophy, the human sciences, the arts, and literature, and the personal experience of the preacher. In setting up this conversa-

61. Ibid., 22.
62. Tracy, *Blessed Rage*, 32.
63. Ibid., 43.
64. Ibid., 46.
65. Allen, "Preaching as Mutual Critical Correlation."

tion, the preacher takes a mutual critical correlational approach: She "not only identifies today's questions to which the tradition gives answer, but also criticizes the contemporary world from the perspective of the gospel; at the same time, the preacher criticizes the Christian tradition from the perspective of contemporary insights and experiences."[66] Allen recognizes that the Bible, given its proven power to invoke a sense of the presence and leading of God, should not be viewed as simply one voice taking its place alongside all the rest. But neither does he wish to exempt it from criticism. This is a method of *mutual critical* correlation. While the other sources may show us where the Bible is particularly helpful, they may also point to parts where it is particularly unhelpful. Here is an example of Allen's approach:

> John 8:39–47 denies that certain Jewish people are children of Sarah and Abraham but are, instead, descendants of the devil. This text denies God's love for these people. The sermon conversation needs to name the theological inadequacy of this text and expose its ideological (anti-Jewish) bias.[67]

If a preacher is going to be responsible in the way she makes judgments such as this one, she will obviously need clear, theologically sound guidelines. Allen, following theologian Clark Williamson, suggests three such guidelines—namely, appropriateness to the gospel, intelligibility, and moral plausibility.[68] These terms need brief explication in order for their meaning to be clear. The gospel is construed by Allen, again following Williamson, as "the promise of God's unconditional love for each and every entity and the call of God for justice . . ."[69] In the example above, the John 8 passage is adjudged to require critique because it constitutes a denial of God's love for the Jewish people in question. To preach in a way that is intelligible, second, means essentially building a bridge from the world of the Bible to the contemporary world. It requires provision of relevant background information, translation of certain concepts so that they make sense to the modern person, and maintenance of logical consistency in engaging with the diversity found in sacred scripture. Moral plausibility, lastly, connects with the fundamental principle enunciated in the first guideline. The preacher needs to ask whether or not the text that is the focus of the sermon

---

66. Ibid., 9.

67. Ibid., 11.

68. See Williamson, *Way of Blessing*, 29–32.

69. Allen, "Preaching as Mutual Critical Correlation," 10.

supports core gospel values. The question, then, is this: Does this text invite us to treat all people with justice and as objects of God's unconditional love?

This, then, in a nutshell is Allen's approach to mutual critical correlation in preaching. There are clearly some questions that could be legitimately raised in relation to this model. For instance, is Allen's understanding of the essential nature of the gospel an adequate one? There is, for example, no specific reference to the word of the cross and to sin and grace—categories that many take to be at the center of the gospel. Then there is the fact that Allen assumes that the biblical world must be interpreted in such a way as to be intelligible to the modern person. But this could be turned around. Perhaps the way the modern person thinks needs to be changed in some crucial respects in order to fit with the biblical worldview. We will return to the model below when we look at dangers associated with correlational preaching. The question that is most pressing at this point is this: Does mutual critical correlation feature in the model of therapeutic preaching being proposed here? The answer is simply that it will in some cases. It is not that the correlational work must in all instances be mutual and critical. It may be that a piece of psychotherapeutic psychology suggests that something in the text is not particularly helpful in the contemporary context. I appreciate that behind this statement stands a particular theological stance. I align myself with the approach to the Bible that distinguishes between the eternal message and the culturally determined, time-limited one. The real issue in relation to this approach is, of course, which parts of the Bible should be assigned to the first category, and which parts to the second. Addressing this issue is beyond the scope of the present work. It perhaps suffices to say that in my view psychotherapeutic psychology may be legitimately used to critique a portion of Scripture that is deemed both to be culturally determined and unhelpful in the present social and cultural context.

Already a red flag will have been raised for some readers. In their judgment, a non-theological discipline is being granted a status that it has no valid right to. There are a number of other objections that can be raised in relation to the method of correlation in general, and to correlational preaching in particular. It is to these that we now turn.

Dealing With Potential Problems
with Correlational Preaching

We have already seen that Tillich himself identifies potential pitfalls in the method of correlation. Recall that he observes that "whenever a philosophy of religion [is] used as an entering door into the theological system . . . the problem [arises] of how far the door determines the structure of the house, or the house the door."[70] In respect of the first part of Tillich's concern—the door determining the structure of the house—Hans Frei makes a similar observation. He refers to the problem of "the great reversal" effected by the "mediating theologians." For this group of theologians, interpretation is "a matter of fitting the biblical story into another world with another story rather than incorporating that world into the biblical story."[71] This is clearly a strong challenge. Let us at this point put it to our three theologians. Does Schleiermacher, first, lose touch with the biblical story when he grounds religious experience in an aesthetic intuition of the universe? Feeling and self-awareness are indeed central values in the Romantic movement, but they seem to be a very long way from the gospel message of Christ as the bearer of the reign of God in which sin, death, and injustice are overcome. Schleiermacher clearly moves much closer to the world of the Bible in his systematic theology in which Christ is construed as the bearer of perfect God-consciousness. But there is a strong argument to be made that immediate awareness of absolute dependence says more about Schleiermacher's Romanticist and philosophical commitments than it does about the story of Israel and of Jesus.

Let us now turn our attention to Tillich's system. Is it the case that his ontological categories and elements take us into that world in which God graciously encounters Israel and the church? Or does his existentialist analysis carry us off into another world altogether? Does the notion of Christ as bearer of the New Being put us firmly in biblical territory? Or is Tillich guilty of making the Gospel proclamation of the Christ event fit his existentialist categories? The answers to these questions are clearly dependent on one's theological stance. A Barthian or a postliberal theologian would answer the last question in the affirmative. A correlational theologian—or at least one sympathetic to existentialist philosophy—would counter the criticism by arguing that Tillich has creatively drawn a connecting line between the *kerygma* and the pressing existential concerns of humans.

70. Tillich, *ST II*, 14.

71. Frei, *Eclipse of Biblical Narrative*, 130.

We turn lastly to Rahner's work on faith as courage. Recall that he refers to the absolute hope associated with the courage required to face up to the challenge of self-realization. He correlates revealed faith with this profound experience of hope. While some will see here a creative re-interpretation of faith, others will argue that Rahner's treatment distorts the true meaning of the biblical term—namely, radical trust in God's justifying work in and through Christ.

Behind the second guideline for mutual critical correlation in preaching provided by Ronald Allen—viz., intelligibility—is the assumption that the concepts, symbols, and language in the text that is the focus of the sermon need to be shaped to accord with the worldview of the modern person. He contends that the sermon "needs to ask the congregation to believe and do things that are intelligible in the contemporary world."[72] Tillich clearly has this in mind in his sermon, "You are Accepted." "Sin" and "grace," as we saw above, are deemed to be strange words for the modern person. Two new words—words that are likely to be immediately meaningful for the twentieth-century person—are proffered: "alienation" and "acceptance." The very clear danger here is that in the translation exercise the inner meaning of the text is partially or even totally lost. What Frei and the other narrative theologians plead for is entry into the biblical world on its own terms. In this approach, the biblical narratives are construed as realistic, as "history-like." Frei refers to the "curious, unmarked frontier between history and realistic fiction" that one finds in the Bible.[73] The interpreter of the Bible should aim to "set forth a temporal world," as this is the way in which the realistic narratives make sense. Here, of course, we hear an echo of Barth's famous call to bravely enter "the strange world of the Bible." From this perspective, it is deemed that the correlational preacher runs a very real risk of constructing her own world. The concepts from the cultural self-interpretations that she employs, far from illuminating the deeper meaning of the symbols in the text, actually distort it. The biblical narrative is twisted out of shape in order to meet the taste, interests, and assumptions of the modern person. What about, inquires the narrative theologian, telling the biblical stories in all their depth and power so that the modern person is formed *by them*?

The problem of "the great reversal" is a real one for the preacher employing a correlational approach. There is an ever-present temptation to

---

72. Allen, "Preaching as Mutual Critical Correlation," 11.

73. Frei, *Eclipse of Biblical Narrative*, 150.

allow the concepts from psychology or philosophy to take over. The various parts of the text are manipulated until they align with the contemporary discourse. If the correlational preacher is to avoid this pitfall, she needs to be firmly committed to maintaining the integrity of the text. In her interpretive work, she needs to allow the meaning to unfold rather than forcing it to align with a pre-understanding conditioned by a particular psychological or philosophical theory. The concepts from whatever theory is used are meant to bring out important aspects of the deep inner meaning of the text. The psychological or philosophical theory is the servant of the text, not its master.

Framing the task of the preacher in this way brings me into conflict with the approach that the narrative theologian Mark Ellingsen advocates. He construes the task of theology as describing the character and identity of the world of the Bible. The task of preaching he sees as telling the Bible's stories about that world. Ellingsen contrasts his narrative approach with that of the correlational preacher:

> [W]hen preaching becomes understood as the task of narrating the biblical account, Scripture effectively functions as its own interpreter. It interprets itself insofar as such preaching rejects the imposition of extraneous categories upon itself, and it allows its narratives to speak for themselves.[74]

Ellingsen's argument is that Scripture is self-interpreting; reading it through a lens supplied by an "alien" discipline constitutes a failure to allow it to speak for itself. I contend that provided the lens is appropriate and is properly applied, the text will speak even more clearly than it would in an unaided interpretation. Tillich puts it well: "[The one] who reads Ecclesiastes or Job with eyes opened by existentialist analyses will see more in either than he was able to see before. The same is true of many other passages of the Old and New Testaments."[75] What Tillich says in relation to existentialist thought can, of course, be more widely applied to include other cultural self-interpretations. I am advocating the use of psychotherapeutic psychology as an aid to biblical interpretation because I am convinced that it helps us to grasp an important aspect of the meaning of the text that would otherwise have remained hidden.

74. Ellingsen, *Integrity of Biblical Narrative*, 19.
75. Tillich, *ST II*, 28.

Of course anyone who follows the theological line of Karl Barth will necessarily reject my argument. Barth holds to the absolute primacy of the revealed divine Word; it is the sole source and criterion for theology. He rejects the claim that psychology, philosophy, or any other cultural discipline captures the deep meaning of human existence. The Word alone is illuminating; we are the ones who are illuminated by it. Our sin prevents us from truly understanding who and what we are: "Human sin excludes us from understanding human nature except by a new disclosure through the perception of divine grace addressed to [the human] and revealing and affirming true humanity in the midst of human sin, i.e., a disclosure which is genuinely new, involving faith in the divine revelation."[76] In the end, the rightness or wrongness of this approach is a question of judgment. Schleiermacher, Tillich, Rahner, and the other mediating theologians take the view that, despite their limitations, philosophy and the human sciences do reveal something really important about the nature of human existence. Moreover, it is held that these disciplines have insights that are not fully present in the Scriptures. It is acknowledged that the ideas developed by the philosophers and the psychologists, or at least most of these ideas, are implied in biblical stories and teachings—and sometimes even explicitly dealt with. Freud's notion of unconscious conflict, Jung's archetypes, the existentialist concepts of estrangement, meaninglessness, guilt, and despair, and more can all be found in either implicit or explicit form in the Bible. According to correlational theologians, what the cultural self-interpretations provide is an alternative way of interpreting the basic existential categories that the biblical writers knew about. The alternative development of the categories is grounded in sophisticated and penetrating analysis. Barth looks at these analyses and simply comments that sometimes they confirm in a general way the insights provided by the revealed Word. This is to be expected, and it is not particularly exciting. It is interesting to observe the correspondence, but the theologian does not need to have her work confirmed by cultural self-interpretations:

> [Theological anthropology] has led to statements which are very similar to those in which humanity is described from a very different angle (e.g., by the pagan Confucius, the atheist L. Feuerbach, and the Jew M. Buber) . . .We need not be surprised that there are approximations and similarities. Indeed, in this very fact we may even see a certain confirmation of our results—a confirmation

76. Barth cited in Harrison, "Correlation and Theology," 71.

which we do not need and which will not cause us any particular excitement . . .[77]

This statement points up the essential difference in the approaches of a Barthian and a correlationalist. The correlationalist *does* get excited when she finds lines of connection between a Christian symbol and a piece of cultural self-interpretation. Moreover, she contends that for her work to be relevant she needs to correlate it with the questions and answers that the creative thinkers in the culture are generating. Schleiermacher was strongly of the view that the "cultured despisers" of religion could be reached by a theology that based itself in their cherished notions of aesthetic intuition and the identity of the finite and the infinite. Similarly, Tillich and Rahner (and others) were deeply convinced that the thinking person of the twentieth century needed to hear the gospel presented in existentialist terms. While it is true that it is most often the case that only a relatively small number of people in a given congregation on a Sunday morning are well-versed in contemporary psychological and philosophical thinking, the majority have sucked in the air surrounding these disciplines. That is, they think in the general categories provided by the psychologists and the philosophers. Terms such as unconscious thought, repression, self-actualization, alienation, angst, meaninglessness, and despair float around in their consciousness. The correlational preacher does not accept the view that these categories do not need to be explicitly addressed. She does not accept that simply telling the biblical story creates its own relevance. It is the contention of the correlational preacher that explicitly drawing lines between the experience and thought of those inhabiting the contemporary and the biblical worlds is an indispensable contribution to a meaningful and impacting sermon.

In the end, all this is of course a matter of judgment. Some preachers will be strongly drawn to the idea that the two worlds need to be correlated. Others will support Frei and the narrative preachers who follow him in the contention that correlation in theology (and preaching) results in the "the great reversal" that is so lamentable. Those who take this line argue for Scripture as self-interpreting; psychology or any other non-theological discipline is considered to be alien to the world of the Bible. My view, clearly, is that creative cultural self-interpretations—in the present context, those of the psychologists and the psychotherapists—can be very profitably employed. But I also recognize the force in the counterarguments. It is easy—frighteningly so—to apply the psychological concepts irresponsibly and so

77. Barth cited in Harrison, "Correlation and Theology," 71.

to distort the inner meaning of the text. In the final chapter, examples of the kind of preaching that I am advocating are offered. The reader must judge to what extent I have been able to guard against the potential pitfalls associated with correlational preaching.

The kind of correlational work in preaching that I am proposing has a particular form. The aim is to find in psychotherapeutic theory suitable analogues to the divine *therapeia* that features in the text. It is often assumed that "metaphor" and "analogy" are interchangeable terms. It is to a discussion of the role of therapeutic metaphors and analogues in preaching that we now turn.

5

Metaphors, Analogues, and Therapeutic God-Talk

RECALL THAT THERE ARE two major propositions associated with the model of therapeutic preaching that is presented in this book. The first is that therapeutic preaching is properly understood as pointing listeners to the divine *therapeia*. The second proposition is that counseling theory has an important role to play in preaching divine healing. When an appropriate text presents itself, counseling psychology can be employed to fund analogues that are not only illustrative of God's therapeutic action portrayed in the Scripture passage, but which also have the power to stimulate openness to that therapeutic action. That is to say, the analogical theology in the sermon is not simply didactic; it is also catalytic of deeper openness to divine *therapeia*.

In the previous paragraph, I have used the terms "analogues" and "analogical theology" quite deliberately. I purposely did not refer to "metaphors" and "metaphorical theology." It is sometimes assumed that "metaphor" and "analogy" are simply two different terms for the same thing. In fact, while they do have something in common, they can also be clearly distinguished. Metaphor is a non-logical form of figurative language, while analogy is a logical form. That is, metaphor involves a twist in the semantic field. There is a logical opposition between the idea and its image. In the metaphorical statement, "God is a rock," it is the semantic impertinence or clash that is set up through referring to the Creator, Governor, and Redeemer of the world as a hard, material substance that gives the metaphor its power. It is precisely this logical opposition that is absent in analogy. Analogy has more than one form, but if we take the classical one—namely, proportional analogy—which has the structure a:b as c:d, we will see immediately that this is the case. Using this analogical structure, we can say that God is to the protection of the believer as a rock is to a person hiding from enemies. There is no semantic impertinence here; rather, what we have is a logical explanation of the strange claim that God is a rock.

In what follows, we will see that this distinction is important in relation to the approach that I take to the use of counseling theory in therapeutic preaching, viz., one that aims at leading listeners into a deeper understanding of and openness to divine *therapeia*. Counseling theory is useful for funding analogues to the divine therapy that is expressed in a text. While therapeutic metaphors may be profitably used, the main burden of the imagistic work in the kind of therapeutic sermon that I envision is analogical.

A debate has been going on for a very long time between Roman Catholic and Protestant theologians over the right understanding of analogical God-talk. Two main approaches have been proposed—namely, *analogia entis* (the analogy of being) and *analogia fidei* (the analogy of faith). In very general terms, the analogy of being assigns primacy to knowledge of the being of God, while the analogy of faith privileges knowledge of the action of God received through faith. While some Protestant theologians flatly reject the analogy of being, I will argue below that it is appropriate to incorporate it into theological reflection, as long as it is subordinated to the analogy of faith. I will further argue that when we use therapeutic analogues in pastoral preaching, it is proper to take our lead from the analogy of faith (faithful proclamation of the divine *therapeia* through qualified words—words that bear a likeness to the divine reality to which they point), but also to incorporate the analogy of being (reference to the way the loving being-with that is both the cornerstone of authentic therapy and part of the essential nature of human being is expressed, gives us a revealing glimpse—it can only ever be a glimpse—of God's healing and acceptant love). It will be noted that here primacy is assigned to God in the analogical relation. In using therapeutic analogues in a sermon, a preacher needs to be careful lest she give the impression that her message is that God is like a therapist. Rather, what needs to shape her approach in sermon preparation and delivery is the notion that God's *therapeia* is the condition of the possibility of all human therapy.

The chapter has the following structure. There is first a discussion of the role of metaphor in God-talk in which the distinction between metaphor and analogy is drawn. The reason that the biblical writers, theologians, and preachers use analogy and metaphor—indeed, *must* use these devices—is because God is infinite, invisible, transcendent and therefore beyond the reach of literal language. Following the discussion on metaphorical God-talk is a description of some classic approaches to the incomprehensibility of God. This prepares the way for an exploration of analogical God-talk. There we will see that *analogia fidei* is associated with an affirmative theology founded on the confidence faith has that God has come to us, thereby revealing God's nature and purpose for humanity in and through Christ. The final section consists of an outline of the basic principles that emerge from this discussion of analogical theology pertaining to the responsible use of therapeutic analogues in preaching.

Metaphors and God-Talk

The fundamental problem that theology is faced with is that it must speak about that which is transcendent. God is infinite and invisible, and therefore ultimately beyond the reach of human thought and language. The biblical writers attest to this basic fact concerning God in relation to humanity:

> Then Manoah said to the angel of the Lord, "What is your name, so that we may honor you when your words come true?" But the angel of the Lord said to him, "Why do you ask my name? It is too wonderful" (Judg 13:17–18).

> For as the heavens are higher than the earth, so are my ways higher than your ways and my thoughts than your thoughts (Isa 55:9).

In order to say something about this God who is infinite, invisible, and transcendent, the biblical writers and theologians turn to metaphors. But this is not a case of using poetic, decorative expressions to say something about the being and nature of God that could be said in plain language. Aristotle's contention that what is said metaphorically can also be said literally[1] is highly arguable. Modern philosophers of metaphor aver that human thought, language, and action are fundamentally metaphorical in nature. Lakoff and Johnson have demonstrated that we structure our everyday lives through a series of metaphors.[2] We say, for example, that argument is war: "Your claims are *indefensible*"; "She *attacked every weak point* in my argument"; "He *shot down* all my arguments." But we do not simply refer to

1. See Aristotle, *Poetics*, XXII.7.
2. See Lakoff and Johnson, *Metaphors*, esp. 3–8.

argument as war. The way that we argue is structured to a degree by the concept of war. This means that when it comes to intellectual and artistic endeavors, it is not that metaphors are used in order to decorate what would otherwise be dull and prosaic expression. We simply cannot express truth in the natural sciences, the human sciences, and poetry and literature without recourse to metaphors. Human intellectual and artistic pursuits are only valuable to the extent that they reach beyond that which is known. Scientists, philosophers, and poets explore new territory, break new ground; that is their contribution to the human community. These thinkers and artists are always grasping for that which is beyond their grasp. They are confronted with something that is unfamiliar to them and they therefore do not have the concepts or the language to catch hold of it.

"God" sits at the extreme end of the problem of unfamiliarity. God is invisible, immortal, incorporeal, and perfect—in short, everything that we are not. God is not within our intellectual and linguistic grasp. All theology is therefore necessarily metaphorical. "Since God is not part of the conventional, mundane, fallen Creation, God can be discussed adequately only in language that opens us to the unconventional and extraordinary."[3] As Sallie McFague observes, metaphor gives us a way of speaking about something that is unfamiliar to us through something that is familiar: "[A] metaphor is seeing one thing *as* something else, pretending 'this' is 'that' because we do not know how to think or talk about 'this,' so we use 'that' as a way of saying something about it. Thinking metaphorically means spotting a thread of similarity between two dissimilar objects, events, or whatever, one of which is better known than the other, and using the better-known one as a way of speaking about the lesser known."[4] God is the "this" that we do not know how to talk about, so we use metaphors such as ruler, judge, mother, father, and redeemer to fund our God-talk. All of these terms are very familiar to us; they are drawn from our personal and communal history and experience. Where else could we turn in order to talk about the divine? There is no fund of pure God-language out there; there is no semantic pool that has been set up solely for the purpose of speaking about God. All that we have for our God-talk are the terms and concepts that come from our human experience. Theology is necessarily metaphorical. In metaphorical expression, it is not identity but a relation of similarity and dissimilarity that is posited. As Aristotle puts it in his *Poetics*, "to make good metaphors implies an eye for

3. Zimany, *Vehicle for* God, 58–59.
4. McFague, *Metaphorical Theology*, 15.

resemblances [among dissimilars]."[5] Thus, when we say that God is mother, we do not mean to say that God is a mother without remainder, but rather that God's mode of relating to human beings shares some of the characteristics of mothering.[6]

If one essential characteristic of metaphorization is the perception of similarity between two dissimilar terms, another is the logical absurdity that it entails. This has not always been clearly seen by philosophers of metaphor. Aristotle states that "metaphor is the application of an alien name by transference either from genus to species, or from species to genus, or from species to species, or by analogy, that is, proportion."[7] His theory of metaphor is essentially one of substitution: the image has replaced an absent but ordinary word. So in relation to the metaphorical expression, "His lawyer is a shark," the word "aggressive" has been replaced by the more poetic or decorative one, "shark." The work of Richards,[8] Black,[9] Beardsley,[10] Ricoeur[11] and others on metaphor, however, has overturned this approach. Following Richards' lead, the theory of interaction has been adopted as the most adequate understanding of what happens in metaphorization. According to Richards, "When we use a metaphor, we have two thoughts of different things active together and supported by a single word or phrase, whose meaning is a resultant of their interaction."[12]

Beardsley and Ricoeur have pointed out that the nature of this interaction is one of logical opposition. That is, there is an inherent tension between the two terms in the metaphorical relation. Beardsley uses the example of "the spiteful sun."[13] Two terms that are logically opposed—the sun and spite—are brought into a relation of similarity. It is not logically possible to attribute to a star an emotional expression such as spite. Only human beings (and animals?) can express spitefulness. The genius in this particular metaphor is to perceive that the destructive effects of a burning

---

5. Aristotle, *Poetics*, XXII.9.

6. Cf. McFague, *Models of God*, 22.

7. Aristotle, *Poetics*, XXI.4.

8. See Richards, *Philosophy of Rhetoric*.

9. See Black, *Models and Metaphors*.

10. See Beardsley, "Metaphorical Twist."

11. See Ricoeur, *Rule of Metaphor*.

12. Richards, *Philosophy of Rhetoric*, 93.

13. Beardsley, "Metaphorical Twist," 299.

sun on people, flora, fauna, and soil in a parched area can be likened to a spiteful action. The logical opposition makes for the "metaphorical twist."

Ricoeur uses the term "semantic clash"[14] to describe this logical opposition that is at the core of metaphorization. He points out that the difference between a simile and a metaphor is that only in the case of the latter is there a semantic clash.[15] Ricoeur uses the example of the simile, "Jim is as stubborn as a mule," to make his point. All the words retain their meaning in this figure of speech. The representations "Jim," "stubborn," and "mule" remain distinct and coexist without dissonance. That is, there is no incompatibility between the semic units of the sentence. But "the perception of incompatibility is essential to the interpretation of the message in the case of metaphor."[16] In the expression, "Jim is an ass," there is this semantic clash. There is a semic incompatibility between "Jim" and "ass."

The clearest explication of the metaphorical twist that I have found is provided by Mary Gerhart and Allan Russell.[17] They use visual images to aid their explanatory work. Metaphor is contrasted with analogy: only in the case of the former is there any twisting of logic. The authors ask us to imagine a map of the world of meanings. This map is drawn on a piece of paper. In the case of analogy, a line is drawn between two locations on the map. Imagine for, for example, that we are dealing with the analogical statement, "In his dialectical approach, Socrates torments the citizens of Athens the way a horsefly torments a horse." There are four terms in play here: Socrates, Athenians, horsefly, and horse. On our map of meanings, we can draw straight lines between the sets of terms that show the flow of the logic of the analogy. That is, a straight line can be drawn between the statements "Socrates is to the Athenians" (A) and "a horsefly is to a horse" (B). The reason that the line is straight is that a logical relation is operating here. We do not have to effect a distortion in the world of meaning to achieve alignment between these two statements. The connecting line between (A) and (B) is the idea of tormenting.

But the matter is very different in the case of the metaphorical statement, "Socrates is a horsefly." There is a logical absurdity involved in suggesting that a man is an insect. The only way that we can achieve an alignment between the two terms is to fold our map of meanings in half

14. Ricoeur, *Rule of Metaphor*, 225.

15. Ibid., 220.

16. Ibid.

17. See Gerhart and Russell, *Metaphoric Process*, 109–20.

so that the half with "Socrates" written on it now sits above the half with "horsefly" written on it. There is no way that we can draw a straight line between the terms. There is non-logic rather than logic in the relationship between them. Through this visual image, Gerhart and Russell vividly express the fact that metaphor creates a twist in the world of meanings.

A moment's reflection will reveal that logical opposition is part of all God-talk. This has to do with the fact that concepts grounded in mortal, finite, limited experience are used to refer to the One who is immortal, infinite, and unlimited. Take, for example, the theological affirmation, God is king. A king exercises his rule over his subjects through his physical presence (he speaks and performs certain actions to prosecute his rule). God is an invisible, non-corporeal entity and therefore has no physical presence. There is therefore "semantic impertinence"[18] pertaining between the terms "God" and "king." The same semantic impertinence is involved in all of the other biblical and theological expressions that are so familiar to us.

Following the suggestion by Gerhart and Russell, it is evident that analogical God-talk can be distinguished from the metaphorical type (we will discuss this more fully below). Metaphorical speech is a non-logical form; analogical speech a logical form. The non-logicality of metaphor has to do with the logical opposition (Beardsley) or semantic clash (Ricoeur) that is its core dynamic. Analogy, on the other hand, works with this logical structure: a:b::c:d (a is to b as c is to d). So we can say that God is to her/his spiritual subjects as a king is to his material subjects. What we have here is a logical explication of the non-logical statement God is king.

Those who discuss analogical God-talk start with the problem of the knowability of God. When one gives some thought to this question, it very quickly becomes clear that there is no literal way of speaking about God. God can only be approached analogically. The question of the knowability of God is thrown into very sharp relief by the proponents of negative theology. For them, God is beyond being, essence, and thought. God is the great abyss, the "No Thing" that human thought and language cannot reach.

I want now to give some space to exploring the thought of two well-known proponents of the *via negativa*—namely, Pseudo-Dionysius and Maximus the Confessor. If in the course of struggling with the unusual formulations of these thinkers the reader is wondering why I have bothered to include them, I ask her or him to bear with me. This material is important

---

18. The term is coined by Jean Cohen in his book, *Structure du langage poétique*. A discussion of it can be found in Ricoeur, *Rule of Metaphor*, 229, 272.

in setting the context for the reflections on analogical theology by significant thinkers such as Thomas Aquinas, Karl Barth, and Eberhard Jüngel.

On the Incomprehensibility of God

The *via negativa* emerged because certain theologians came to a profound awareness of the infinite qualitative distinction between humans beings and God. God is infinite, invisible, and absolutely transcendent. All of the categories that humans work with—space, time, quality, quantity, etc.—simply do not apply to the infinite. Human thought and language are incapable of expressing the being and nature of God. According to the proponents of the *via negativa*, positive affirmations about God will always be misleading. They hinder rather than help us to know God. The one who truly wants to know God will jettison reason and thought and embark on the way of mystical contemplation that leads to union with God.

Pseudo-Dionysius

The incomprehensibility of God is the constant theme in the theology of Pseudo-Dionysius the Areopagite (ca. 500 CE). This Eastern writer presents himself as a convert of Paul the Apostle; Dionysius is a pseudonym. His mystical theology is set within the neoplatonic framework of Plotinus and Proclus. In this spiritual philosophy, the highest principle and creator is absolutely transcendent. Everything that exists, flows from this principle as an emanation and ultimately returns to it. Those engaged in the upward ascent through knowledge contemplate the spiritual forms and have as their ultimate goal mystical union with the source.

The central term in Dionysius's approach to speaking about God is the "Super-Essential God." The Ultimate Godhead is absolutely transcendent; It is totally beyond being and essence, totally beyond reason, thought, and language: "The boundless Super-Essence surpasses Essences, the Super-Intellectual Unity surpasses intelligences, the One which is beyond thought surpasses the apprehension of thought, and the Good which is beyond utterance surpasses the reach of words."[19]

---

19. See Pseudo-Dionysius the Areopagite, *On the Divine Names and the Mystical Theology*, I.1. Hereafter referred to as *DN*.

Dionysius uses the term "Super-Essential" in the sense of transcendence of essence. Essence or being applies to an individual existence—more particularly, to a person. Therefore the Super-Essential Godhead is beyond personhood. The concept of essence can be used to distinguish between different kinds of existents. A horse has a different essence to a human ("horseness" can be distinguished from "humanness"). But God's plane of existence is beyond being: "He is not an attribute of Being, but Being is an Attribute of Him; He is not contained in Being, but Being is contained in Him; He doth not possess Being, but Being possesses Him; He is the Eternity, the Beginning, and the Measure of Existence, being anterior to Essence and essential Existence and Eternity, because He is the Creative Beginning, Middle, and End of all things."[20]

The Super-Essential Godhead is beyond deity as it is beyond existence.[21] There is an impersonal God, the Absolute, beyond the personal God. God is simply the highest manifestation or emanation of the Absolute. There is a close parallel here with that stream of Jewish mysticism known as Kabbalah. Ein Sof (literally, Endlessness) is the name given to the Absolute. Ein Sof is the "great abyss" that is completely beyond the reach of human thought and language. The only path to knowledge of God is through the divine emanations. Ein Sof created the world through a process of emanation and thereby revealed Itself. The emanations are known as the sefiroth, or the "Tree of Life." The term "sefiroth" is difficult to translate. Common interpretations are "attributes," "channels," and "energies." Quite a few of the names of the sefiroth are found in verse 11 in 1 Chronicles 29: "Yours, O Lord, is the greatness [*gedulah*], and the power [*gevurah*], and the beauty [*tiferet*], and the victory [*netzach*], and the majesty [*hod*], for all that is in heaven and on earth."

Kabbalah holds that the problem of the ineffability of Ein Sof is overcome through the Absolute's creative act. God creating is God revealing. Though he does not make the link between creation and revelation in precisely this way, Dionysius also avers that the Ultimate Deity has graciously made itself known. The form of the revelation is sacred Scripture: "[The] mysteries we learn from Divine Scriptures, and thou will find that in well-nigh all the utterances of the Sacred Writers the Divine Names refer in Symbolical Revelation to Its beneficent Emanations."[22] The Emanations that Dionysius refers

20. Pseudo-Dionysius, *DN*, V.8.
21. Cf. Kellenberger, "The Slippery Slope," 46.
22. Pseudo-Dionysius, *DN*, I.4.

to are the creative and redemptive actions of God. In saying that Scripture through its references to divine actions teaches us about the nature of God, Dionysius does not mean to imply that we therefore have anything like full access to that divine nature. The best that Scripture can do—even though it is inspired by the Holy Spirit—is afford us a glimpse of God. The Ultimate Godhead is beyond words and concepts.[23]

Theology proceeds by the negative path. Dionysius says that there is ". . . no more fitting method to celebrate its [Ultimate Godhead's] praises than to deny it every manner of Attribute."[24] Such descriptions of God as invisible, infinite, and ungraspable do not describe what God is, only what God is not. Thus, when Scripture uses terms for God that seem not to fit deity at all, this is entirely appropriate; it shows that the sacred writers fully acknowledge the incapacity of human language to describe God. For this reason, Dionysius declares his warm approval for a verse taken from the Seventy-Eighth Psalm: "The Lord awoke, like a strong man, powerful but reeling with wine."[25] If these terms are taken literally, God sleeps and gets drunk on wine. But these are activities that only an embodied, visible being can engage in. A literal approach obviously ends in absurdity. Dionysius therefore states that we must look to a symbolical meaning. Using analogical reasoning, he suggests that there is a similarity between the human sleep and the divine nature located in the concept of withdrawal from the world. God is like a sleeper in that God does not participate in time and space. The analogue that he finds in relation to drunkenness is the "overloaded measurelessness" of the divine goodness. Just as a drunk is filled to overflowing with wine, so God is filled to overflowing with goods (love, wisdom, truth etc.).

For the same reason, Dionysius is most approving of Paul's saying that "the foolishness of God is wiser than human wisdom" (1 Cor 1:25). To speak literally of the foolishness of God makes no sense; God is infinitely wise. But, says Dionysius, Paul is using "in a higher sense the apparent strangeness and absurdity implied in the word, so as to hint at the ineffable Truth which is before all reason."[26]

---

23. Cf. Beggiani, "Theology at Service of Mysticism," 205.

24. Pseudo-Dionysius, *DN*, I.5.

25. On Dionysius' interpretation of God's "sleep" and "drunkenness," see Corrigan and Harrington, "Pseudo-Dionysius the Areopagite."

26. Pseudo-Dionysius, *DN*, VII.1.

What the Scripture writers affirm, then, is that God is both nameless and known by many names. These names are a celebration of the nameless One. When terms such as "good" and "wise" are applied to God, they do not speak directly to the Ultimate Godhead. They cannot do so because any linguistic utterances will inevitably fall short of Super-Essential deity. What the divine names do is refer to an emanation of the Super-Essential Godhead. So Dionysius says that "it is not the purpose of our discourse to reveal the Super-Essential Being in its Super-Essential Nature (for this is unutterable, nor can we know It, or in anywise express It, and It is beyond even the Unity), but only to celebrate the Emanation of the Absolute Divine Essence into the universe of things."[27]

Maximus the Confessor

Maximus the Confessor (582–662), also known as Maximus of Constantinople, was one of the most important Byzantine theologians. He follows Dionysius's view of God as incomprehensible and beyond essence and being: "God is one, without beginning, incomprehensible . . . unlimited, unmoved, and infinite in that he is infinitely beyond every essence, power, and act."[28] Maximus also endorses the Pseudo-Areopagite's view that the appropriate language for talking about God is a negative one. The way in which Maximus discusses the relationship between a negative and an affirmative theology is built on a distinction he makes between a spirituality of the flesh and a spirituality of the spirit. Those who are beginners on the way to communion with God take an "active" approach. They make the Word of God flesh through concentrating on the concrete concerns of the moral life. This is commendable, but the spiritual progressives move beyond this to a state of mystical contemplation. The contemplatives come to God without any images; they approach God with "a pure mind without sense activity."[29] Maximus aligns negative theology with the purity and wisdom obtained by the contemplatives. The one who speaks of God negatively makes the Word spirit, as he was prior to his incarnation. "Using absolutely nothing which can be known he knows in a better way the utterly Unknowable."[30]

27. Ibid., V.1.

28. *Chapters on Knowledge* I.1 and I.2 in Maximus Confessor, *Maximus Confessor* (hereafter referred to as *CK*).

29. Maximus Confessor, *CK*, 2.59.

30. Ibid., 2.39.

To this point, Maximus sounds just like Dionysius. However, he makes a decisive theological move that the Pseudo-Areopagite could not—namely, from the absolute unknowability of God to a revelation of God in the Word. Paul Rorem sums it up neatly: "Because we cannot know God as transcendent, we look instead to God as incarnate."[31] Maximus speaks of the Word of God as a door and a key to the truth: "He is . . . door and key . . . a key as the one who opens and who is opened for those who are worthy of divine treasures; a door as the one who gives entry . . ."[32]

But the door that is opened can only ever be partially opened. This is not, of course, a result of any limitation pertaining to the Word, but rather one that is in us. In the relations in the Trinity, God the Father knows God the Word through a "clear and naked" apprehension of the truth. Humans, on the other hand, with their "naked mind reach naked spiritual realities."[33] So the Word made flesh communicates with them in a way suited to their limitations by making use of "stories, enigmas, parables, and dark sayings." For this reason, the one who is living within the limitations of this temporal realm can never fully grasp the naked truth of the Word. "Even if he be perfect in his earthly state both in action [i.e., the moral life] and in contemplation, he still has knowledge, prophecy, and the pledge of the Holy Spirit only in part, not in their fullness."[34] The fullness of the truth will only be known when he obtains his eternal glory.

The theologians of the Word such as Karl Barth and Eberhard Jüngel share in the basic affirmation of Maximus that the transcendent One reveals himself/herself through the incarnate Son, but there is an importance difference. This difference has to do with the human capacity to say what God is. The Confessor considers that even with the aid of revelation through the Incarnate One, positive statements about God are misleading. The theologians of the Word, on the other hand, contend that human words can truly say what God is. They do mean thereby to suggest, of course, that it is possible to capture God *in* se (God in God's own self). But in terms of who God is, the Word tells us all we need to know: God is the one who justifies humankind in and through the death of the man Jesus.

---

31. Rorem, "Negative Theologies and the Cross," 460.
32. Maximus Confessor, *CK*, 2.69.
33. Ibid., 2.60.
34. Ibid., 2.87.

Aquinas

Aquinas restates the axiom of the incomprehensibility of God held by Dionysius and Maximus by narrowing its range. Thus, he reiterates the proposition that we cannot cognize the essence of God. In the *Summa Theologiae* I.12.4, Aquinas asks the question: "Is any created intellectual substance sufficient by its own nature to see the essence of God?"[35] His answer is "no." The fundamental reason that Aquinas gives for this is that there is a total disjuncture, an infinite qualitative gap, between the Creator and the created. We know things according to our mode of being. Our mode of being is a material one; God's is immaterial. We can know things that exist on the material plane; we cannot know things that exist on the heavenly plane. It is impossible for a finite mind to cognize that which is infinite.

In article 7, Aquinas asks a similar question to the one above, and that question is this: Can any created intellect comprehend the divine essence? His answer, given what has just been said, can only be that it is impossible for the human intellect to comprehend God. To comprehend something is to know it perfectly. When a thing is known as much as it can be known, then it is known perfectly. Aquinas gives the example of a triangle. Once it is known that a triangle has three angles the sum of which is 180°, the geometrical concept of a triangle is perfectly known. While it is possible to grasp certain finite entities fully, it is not possible to grasp an infinite entity completely. Since God is infinite, God is infinitely knowable. Due to the limitations that a finite intellect is subject to, it cannot know God infinitely. It is therefore impossible to comprehend God. While Aquinas is in agreement with Pseudo-Dionysius and Maximus on this fundamental point, he parts company with them when he says that it is possible to make positive statements about God that are literally true. Proponents of the *via negativa* hold that affirmative theology obscures rather than reveals God's nature. The deepest knowledge of God comes through a mystical union in which words, thoughts, images have all been left behind. Aquinas believes that reason and language have the power to arrive at true knowledge of God. As we shall see below, Thomas uses an analogical approach to the divine names. But while the names of God (God is good, wise, etc.) are said affirmatively and absolutely, they do not

---

35. I have used the translation of the *Summa Theologiae* in the Hackett Aquinas series. See Aquinas, *The Treatise on the Divine Nature: Summa Theologiae I 1–13*. The *Summa* is hereafter referred to in the text as *ST*.

express fully the divine being and nature. Human language can only ever express the divine perfection imperfectly.

God Is Not an "X": Analogy of Being, Analogy of Faith and Analogy of Advent

For Immanuel Kant, to assign attributes such as goodness and wisdom to God is to fall into a "dogmatic anthropomorphism."[36] A basic principle in Kant's epistemology is that a thing can only be known through its appearances (the thing as *phenomenon*); it is not possible to know the thing in itself (the *noumenon*). Kant puts the Supreme Being in the category of *noumena*. Thus, when it comes to God as an object of knowledge, he suggests that we are bound by the limits of our finitude. The concept of God lies beyond the knowledge that is possible in this world. Kant nevertheless states that it is possible to speak meaningfully about this Unknown through what he calls a "symbolic anthropomorphism." This approach "concerns language only and not the object itself."[37] What he means by this is that he intends to speak only analogically concerning God. Further, he limits himself to talking about the relation that the world may have to the Supreme Being. Kant posits that there must be a Supreme Reason that is the condition of the possibility of human reason.[38] That is, there must be some ultimate cause of reason in the world. Things in the world exhibit order, patterns, and cause and effect relations that are discernible by the rational mind. That is, there is a rational ordering of things in the world that is simply a given for us. We did not cause it; it was caused. There is something outside the world that is responsible for the rational order that is everywhere in the world. In speaking in this way, Kant makes it clear that he is not thereby attributing the property of reason to God, but is rather referring to God as the ground of reason. Moreover, he is making this claim through the use of analogical expression: "Nothing is considered here but the cause of the form of reason which is perceived everywhere in the world, and reason is indeed attributed to the Supreme Being so far as it contains the ground of this form of reason in the world, but only according to analogy only—that is, so far as this expression shows merely the relation which the Supreme Cause, unknown

---

36. Kant, *Prolegomena to Any Future Metaphysics*, 105.
37. Ibid., 106.
38. See ibid., 107.

to us, has to the world in order to determine everything in it conformably to reason in the highest degree."[39]

The analogical relation between God and the world is an "as if" relation. That is, Kant contends that "we conceive the world *as if* it came, in its existence and internal plan, from a Supreme Reason."[40] Such an approach has two advantages. On the one hand, says Kant, we know the constitution of the world (it is rationally ordered) without claiming to know the nature of the cause in itself (God is the Unknown). On the other hand, we offer a cogent explanation of the rational ordering of things in the world by attributing it to the *relation* of the Supreme Cause to the world (all that we are able to determine *vis-à-vis* God is God's relation to the world).

Kant makes use of the analogy of proportion in describing the relation between God and the world. As we have seen, this kind of analogy has the form: a:b::c:d. The analogues that he works with are watch/watchmaker, ship/shipbuilder, regiment/commanding officer, on the one hand, and world of sense/Unknown (i.e., God), on the other. If we use the first set of material analogues only (watch/watchmaker), then we see that what Kant is positing in his analogical approach to God is this: A watch is to a watchmaker as the world of sense is to the Unknown.

Kant says of analogy that it is "a perfect similarity of relations between two quite dissimilar things."[41] Thus, by the use of analogy it is possible to obtain an understanding of the relation of things which are completely unknown to one:

> For instance, as the promotion of welfare of children (=a) is to the love of parents (=b), so the welfare of the human species (=c) is to that unknown character in God (=x), which we call love; not as if it had the least similarity to any human inclination, but because we can suppose its relation to the world to be similar to that which things of the world bear one another.[42]

Thus, we can reformulate Kant's analogy as a:b::c:x. God is an "X" for humans. We are at much the same place as that of Dionysius and Maximus. God is ultimately beyond the reach of human thought, reason, and language. God is the great abyss, the No Thing, the incomprehensible and ineffable One.

39. Ibid.
40. Ibid., 108.
41. Ibid., 106.
42. Ibid., 106n1.

Aquinas's solution to the problem of the incomprehensibility of God is to use an analogical approach that allows positive affirmations about the nature and being of God, while acknowledging that the essence of God always remains hidden. This latter position is central in a discussion on the name-ability of God in the *Summa Theologiae*.[43] He inquires as to whether or not it is within the capability of human beings to name God. In the dialectical style that characterizes the *Summa*, Aquinas begins with a position that is diametrically opposed to his own. Pseudo-Dionysius states in the first chapter of *On Divine Names* that "of God there is neither name nor opinion." In reply, Aquinas acknowledges that the human intellect cannot cognize the essence of God. However, he adds that it is possible to know God from creatures, to the extent that God is the source of our mode of being in the world. Taking this path, it is possible to name God but not in such a way that the name expresses the essence of God as it really is. The name "human being" expresses the essence of being human, but any name for God that we may choose can never define the essence of God. Any name will necessarily fall short of God's own mode of being because the cognizing power of the human intellect cannot extend beyond the realm of the finite.

Despite this fact that any naming of God is necessarily deficient, Aquinas is convinced that an analogical approach does allow us to speak meaningfully about the nature and being of God. We observe certain "perfections" in human beings such as goodness, wisdom, and justice. We know that the ultimate source of these is not human but divine. God is the cause of these good effects in us. It is therefore possible to establish an analogical relation between goodness, wisdom, etc., in humans and goodness, wisdom, etc., in God.

A central issue for Aquinas in this regard is the rightful assignment of primacy in the analogical relation. There is a significant development in this respect from his work in the *Summa Contra Gentiles* to his mature position in the *Summa Theologiae*.[44] In the former work he presents what many would take to be a common sense approach: God's perfections have an ontological priority over the human counterparts; but the semantic priority is with humans. This is how he puts it:

> [B]ecause we come to a knowledge of God from other things, the reality in the names said of God and other things belong by priority in God according to His mode of being, but the meaning of

43. Aquinas, *ST,* I.13.1.
44. See White, *Talking about God*, 87.

the name belongs to God by posteriority. And so He is said to be named from His effects.[45]

It seems a common sense approach to refer to human perfections having a linguistic priority over divine ones. As a person's vocabulary develops, she learns about the meaning of terms such as goodness, wisdom, and justice in their human context first. Parents and other teachers tell her about the meaning of the words "good," "wise," and "just" through reference to human agents and events. In addition, she has personal experiences of these virtues in action. Gradually the meaning of the terms as they pertain to human existence becomes clear to her. Subsequently, she learns how to apply the names "goodness," "wisdom," etc., to God; she thinks of these as the divine attributes.

In the *Summa Theologiae*, however, Aquinas claims that the priority in the analogical relation is with God both in an ontological *and* in a linguistic sense. It is clear that God expresses goodness, wisdom, and the other perfections perfectly; we express them only imperfectly. This is because God has them originally and perfectly and infuses them into us. As a result of our finite, sinful nature we are not able to receive them in all their fullness. Therefore it is clearly appropriate to assign the ontological priority to God. But Aquinas goes further than this. He contends that linguistic priority is also with God. What he means by this is that the true meaning of the term "goodness," for example, is found in God's manifestation of it. That is, the goodness of God is the measure against which all human expressions are judged.

He presents his thinking on this in his discussion of the issue of metaphorical naming of God.[46] He notes, first, that in general a name is said primarily of some things and secondarily of others. Aquinas uses the example of health.[47] The name "healthy" is assigned primacy in the statement: "This animal is healthy." It is said secondarily of both medicine and urine. The term "healthy" enters into medicine in that the medicine has restored the animal to a healthy state. Similarly, "healthy" is associated with the animal's urine because certain characteristics of it indicate good health.

Aquinas contrasts his analogical approach to that of Pseudo-Dionysius, for example, in which God is named from creatures (God is king, a lion, etc.). That difference is that a metaphorical naming of God means that God is assigned a secondary status:

45. The translation I have used is by Pegis. See Aquinas, *On the Truth*, I.34.6.
46. Aquinas, *ST*, I.13.3 and I.13.6.
47. Ibid., I.13.6.

> All the names that are said metaphorically of God are said primarily of creatures rather than of God, since what is said of God in this way signifies nothing other than a likeness to such creatures. For just as to say that a meadow is smiling signifies nothing other than that it is similar in beauty when it flowers to a person who smiles, according to some likeness of proportion, so too the name "lion" when said of God signifies just that God is the sort of being that acts powerfully in his works, just as a lion is. So it is clear that when these terms are said of God, their signification cannot be defined except through what is said of creatures.[48]

We would be no further along, according to Thomas, in the case of names "not said metaphorically of God" (i.e., those said analogically), if they were only said causally of God. For if when we say God is good we meant nothing other than that God is the cause of goodness in creatures, then the term "good" as said of God would be first and foremost a reference to something that creatures have. That is, it would be said primarily of creatures and secondarily of God. But Aquinas argues that the analogical names of God are said of God not only causally but also essentially. God is not only the cause of goodness and wisdom, but these are prepossessed by God in a perfect way. The essence of the Godhead is goodness, and it is therefore in the essential nature of God to diffuse what God is to the created order. "Accordingly, it should be said that with respect to the thing signified by the name, it is said primarily of God rather than creatures, since perfections of this kind flow from God to creatures."[49] Thus, while it is true that the basis for analogical theology is human experience—it cannot be otherwise because we cannot comprehend the essence of God—the flow in its logic is ultimately from God down rather than from creatures up.

What Aquinas is doing with his analogical approach is to show that the poetic language of worship can be demonstrated to be rational and intelligible. His approach involves giving attention to the linguistic rules associated with analogical theology.[50] Thomas draws a distinction between "what is signified" and our "mode of signifying." In using a word we refer to a particular thing—this is what is signified by the particular name we use. The mode of signification, on the other hand, refers to what we can know of the thing that is referred to. Thus, when we, for example, assign

48. Ibid.

49. Ibid.

50. On Aquinas's analogical theology as a linguistic approach, see Lash, "Ideology, Metaphor and Analogy"; and DeHart, "On Being Heard."

the term "good" to God, we are saying something of God that is literally true—that is, we are correctly signifying God's very essence—but this not to be taken to mean that we are able to close the infinite gap separating time and eternity. In saying that reference to God in terms of goodness and wisdom constitutes a proper or literal reference, Aquinas is not thereby meaning to imply that we can fully comprehend goodness and wisdom as God experiences these perfections in God's self. Paul DeHart sums up Aquinas' general approach well:

> Perfection terms ["goodness," wisdom" etc.] can "refer" to God literally because, ontologically, God contains all perfection eminently, but also because, semantically, some of our perfection terms have meanings which do not explicitly connote finitude. Nonetheless, we cannot know the perfection of God through the literally correct application of those terms, because even though the "*ratio*" [meaning] signified by the word has no limit annexed semantically to it, the mode of signifying of human users of the word inevitably does involve such limitation.[51]

The theology of the Word approach, by way of contrast, has been to employ *analogia fidei*. In this approach, participation in the being of God through faith is given priority over knowledge of the being of God. As Eberhard Jüngel puts it: "Revelation is, in its facticity, not primarily an occasion for knowledge, but rather an event of self-sharing in the being of the one revealing himself, an event which implies knowledge. Accordingly, faith is not primarily a mode of knowing but rather an event of human participation in the being of that one who allows such participation in his being . . ."[52] It is this event in which God communicates God's being through coming to the world in Christ that overcomes "God as x". Jüngel formulates it this way: if "a" stands for the world, then x → a replaces x:a. He goes on to state that: "In the event of the analogy x→a=b:c God ceases to be x. He introduces himself in that he arrives. And this his arrival belongs to his very being which he reveals as arriving."[53] Jüngel refers to his approach as an "analogy of advent."[54] The central act associated with God's arrival is the "word of the cross." The word of the cross is an event that expresses the fact of God's unity with the man Jesus who died on the cross, and the

51. DeHart, "On Being Heard," 270.

52. Jüngel, *God as Mystery of the World*, 228.

53. Ibid., 286.

54. Ibid.

distinction between God and humanity, and that achieves the justification of the human person in her or his being as human.[55] Thus, this word is a proclamation that allows God to speak definitively. The word of the cross is the event of the self-communication of God. The human words that surround this word of love communicate what God is. The proponents of the *via negativa*, along with Kant, contend that the God outside the world cannot be spoken about. But according to Jüngel, "If God is one who justifies [humanity], then that is already a statement about who or what God is. For justification requires recognition. Recognition, however, requires that the one who is recognized *permit* himself to be recognized. Therefore justification takes place solely on the basis of faith."[56]

This address of God that is acknowledged in faith is also at the center of Karl Barth's approach to the question of the knowability of God. Barth observes that while in one sense this is a real question, ultimately it is superfluous.[57] It is superfluous because the ground of all human knowledge of God is the knowledge that God has of God's self. This divine self-knowledge consists of the fact that the Father knows the Son and the Son knows the Father by the Holy Spirit.[58] This self-knowledge is perfect knowledge. God knows the divine being and action absolutely, completely. God is infinitely knowable and God knows God's self infinitely. But this perfect knowledge has not remained locked up inside the Godhead. God has graciously chosen to communicate this knowledge to us. That is, we know God because God has revealed God's self through the Word and in the power of the Holy Spirit. Barth acknowledges, of course, that there can be no question of a direct transfer of knowledge from God to humanity. Our experience of revelation is "not immediate but mediated."[59] Therefore, it is inevitable that this knowledge of God which is perfectly known by God is known by us only imperfectly.

According to Barth, that God is knowable cannot in any way be attributed to the human power of thought that starts with the general question of being and then proceeds to comprehend something of God's being. The movement of our own thought that reaches up for God is empty. God

---

55. Ibid., 289.

56. Ibid., 231.

57. See Barth, *Church Dogmatics* II.1, 69. The *Dogmatics* is hereafter referred to in the text as *CD*.

58. Barth, *CD*, II.1, 70.

59. Ibid., II.1, 69.

is knowable because, and only because, the Word has been addressed to us (Jüngel's "analogy of advent"). That is to say, our knowledge of God starts and finishes with the divine initiative—an initiative that is an expression of grace:

> The fact that God is revealed to us is . . . grace . . . Grace is God's good-pleasure. And it is precisely in God's good-pleasure that the reality of our being with God and of His being with us consists. For it is Jesus Christ who is God's revelation, and the reality of this relationship in Jesus Christ is the work of the divine good-pleasure. God's revelation breaks through the emptiness of the movement of thought which we call our knowledge of God. It gives to this knowledge another side, seen from which it is not self-deception but an event in truth, because it happens by the truth.[60]

Barth contends that if the Word is to be knowable through the gracious event of divine revelation, there are two essential requirements.[61] First, the human person must be conformed to the Word of God. That is, there must be an adaptation of the human person to the Word. The human needs to have a capacity to receive God's Word. The second essential requirement is that there must be acknowledgement of the Word of God. This acknowledgment is the event of faith. Neither conformity to the Word nor faith in Christ—in their most fundamental and primary senses—are acts of the human person. An adaptation to the Word and faith in the Word are, in Barth's terminology, received "on loan" from God. They are therefore the result of the free grace of God. It is true that the human person experiences the Word of God, decides in faith for it, and is determined by it. But this experience, this decision, this self-determination are all determined ultimately and absolutely by God. Barth puts it this way: "In faith it is true, accepted and acknowledged acknowledgment, not because man himself has the power or he himself has been able to achieve this proper acknowledgment, but because what he can do and does is acknowledged by the acknowledged Word of God, not as self-determination but as the self-determination determined by God's Word."[62]

In the *Dogmatics*, Barth rejects the method of *analogia entis* because it places God and humanity together on the plane of being. An analogous relation at the level of being—goodness, wisdom, etc.—is established between humanity and God. Barth argues that the analogy is more properly

60. Ibid., II.1, 75.
61. Ibid., I.1, 239, 242.
62. Ibid., I.1, 230.

established on the level of act—viz., the act of God in coming to humanity and the act of faith through which this revelation is acknowledged.

Barth's point is that through faith—which is ultimately an event that is only possible because of the free grace of God—the Word of God is acknowledged, known, thought, and spoken about. The thoughts and words that arise in and through the faith encounter with the Word constitute a similarity, a likeness, an analogy to that Word. Barth, in contrasting the analogy of faith with the analogy of being, expresses it thus:

> Our reply to the Roman Catholic doctrine of *analogia entis* is not, then, a denial of the concept of analogy. We say rather that the analogy in question is not an *analogia entis* but according to Rom. 126 the αναλογία της πίστεως [analogy of faith], the likeness of the known in the knowing, of the object in thought, of the Word of God in the word that is thought and spoken by man, as this differentiates true Christian prophecy in faith from all false prophecy.[63]

What Barth is focusing on here is the relationship between human language and God's speech in revelation.[64] Human language was developed to refer to things and experiences in this world. It is therefore not able in and of itself to serve as a vehicle for God's speech. But because God takes it up and uses it for God's revelatory purpose, it becomes God's Word. Though our words cannot fully express the Word, through the act of faith an analogical relation between the two comes into being. That is, the relationship between human language and God's Word is not one of identity, but one of similitude. "Grace" means something like what God says and does in the election of humanity in and through Christ, in the power of the Holy Spirit.

Barth rejects the use of parallels with human concepts and experience in the quest for knowledge of God because he considers that in the end these parallels are more of a hindrance than a help. The essential problem that Barth sees is that human expressions of lordship, creative activity, redemption, and reconciliation are so vastly different from what is communicated in divine revelation that to pay attention to them in developing one's theology can only result in error and confusion.[65] Barth refers, for example, to the fact that we know of lords in our experience. But to use our experience of human lordship to refer to God the Lord is not efficacious. All that it succeeds in doing is to turn us back on ourselves; it takes us not one inch

63. Ibid., I.1, 244–45.

64. Cf. Bruce L. McCormack, "Barth's Version of an 'Analogy of Being,'" 98–99.

65. Barth, *CD*, II.1, 76–79.

toward a true understanding of the nature of divine rule. Similarly, Barth suggests, we know of originators and causes. But the revealed fact that God is the Creator means something completely different. The Creator means that one alone truly exists and everything else exists as a result of the Creator's will and Word. The notion of creation *ex nihilo* can only be received as something absurd. It is a concept that is absolutely unique; therefore any analogies that we draw based on human experience will lead us away from the Creator rather than toward him. The situation is the same with other possible analogical terms such as reconciliation and redemption. If analogy is to be useful as a theological tool, there needs to be some point of real contact between the human term and the divine being and nature. Barth claims to have shown that no such point exists.

In *Church Dogmatics* II.1 §26, Barth presents more fully his objection to *analogia entis*. His first point is that according to this doctrine, God can be known without revelation.[66] Barth sees in the doctrine the assumption that because the human person is a being, she can know being as such. She can extend this knowledge of being even to the being of the One who absolutely transcends human being. Knowledge of being, then, is considered to be the starting point for a true knowledge of God. Barth finds this unacceptable. His second point of objection is that *analogia entis* seeks to place God and the human on the same plane of being.[67] But the God who reveals God's self to us is the Creator, Lord, Judge and Redeemer of the world. God is therefore "the origin and boundary of all being." How can this God, asks Barth, be drawn down into our domain of being?

It should be noted that Barth developed his position not so much in opposition to the analogical theology of Thomas Aquinas, but to that of the German Jesuit philosopher-theologian, Erich Przywara.[68] Przywara contends that he has developed an approach that, while different in some important respects to that of Aquinas, is nevertheless in continuity with it.[69] The German theologian has a different understanding of the relationship between essence and existence in the human to that of Thomas. Essence is what a thing is. Przywara has a dynamic understanding of the essence of a

66. Ibid., II.1, 82.

67. Ibid., II.1, 84.

68. On the dialogue between Barth and Przywara, see Betz, "Beyond the Sublime"; Oakes, "The Question of Nature and Grace"; and Johnson, "Reconsidering Barth's Rejection."

69. This summary of Przywara's approach to *analogia entis* is drawn from Betz, "Beyond the Sublime," 21–30 and Johnson, "Reconsidering Barth's Rejection," 635–36.

person. That is, he avers that what a person is *qua* human being is not a fixed thing but rather a state of becoming. Essence is immanent in existence, but at the same time it transcends it. Existence, then, is the coming to be of essence. Pryzwara therefore defines human being as "unity-in-tension" of "essence in-and-beyond existence." Essence is in existence (immanence), and it is also beyond it (transcendence). This vocation of becoming that is expressive of the very nature of humans is a participation in the divine life analogically. In the divine life, essence and existence are identical. God expresses the divine essence (love, goodness, and wisdom) fully, perfectly, in the divine mode of being. That is, there is nothing in the divine nature that is not fully actualized. There is no becoming in God; God is Being itself (pure Being). The analogy between the being of God and that of the human person, then, is this. The essence and the existence of a human being form a unity just as God's essence and existence and being do. But this similarity between the human and God contains within it an even greater dissimilarity. Whereas the unity within God is an absolute unity, in the human it is a "unity-in-tension" because essence is not only immanent in existence but also transcends it. In their being, humans express Being (God's being) analogously. God *is* Being; the being of a human person is a participation in Being. Because the being of a human person can only be understood in the context of relationship with God, the human person's existence is itself a revelation of God.

Aquinas also suggests that there is a real distinction between the essence and existence of a human person. He likewise does this to emphasize the very substantial dissimilarity with God. But his way of distinguishing essence and existence does not have the dynamic quality of Pryzwara's approach. Aquinas simply observes that a human being, imperfect being that she is, can never fully express her essential nature through her existence. Goodness is part of the essence of a human being, but in her existence a person is never truly good. What Pryzwara is doing, on the other hand, is positing a dynamic view of essence in order to show that human being is only that which is reaching up for God. The becoming that is the nature of essence is expressed through movement in the direction of God. The human vocation is ever greater conformity to God. Christ is the true image of God (Heb 1:3). Therefore, what a person is (her essence) can only be determined ultimately by her relation to Christ.

Przywara and Barth engaged in an extended dialogue on the role of analogy in theology. In the course of this dialogue, it became obvious to

Przywara that what he thought he was doing in his approach to an *analogia entis* and what Barth thought he was doing were two quite different things. Indeed, in *In Und Gegen*, Pryzwara sees his work—far from representing the antithesis of his interlocutor's approach—as affirming the very values that Barth holds dear.[70] He makes two important points in this regard. The first is that *analogia entis* adopts the principle promulgated at the Fourth Lateran Council in 1215—namely, that in noting any similarity between God and humanity, it is necessary to note an even greater dissimilarity. Thus, *analogia entis* is not a philosophically driven theology in which the created world is ordered to God. It does not therefore attempt to situate God, creation, and creature on the same plane of being. In the theology of both Aquinas and Przywara, God *is* Being; humans simply participate in it. This fact points to God's "dynamic transcendence," according to which God is above and beyond everything that is external to God.

Pryzwara's second point is that the *analogia entis* does not denote a natural theology, but rather operates in the domain of "the supernatural and the genuinely Christian." The primary datum in analogical theology is the perfections of God attested to by Scripture.

We have seen that Barth claims that an *analogia entis* seeks to bypass revelation in developing knowledge of God. In a work published in 1927, Pryzwara explicitly rejects this position: ". . . *analogia entis* means neither a calculation of God nor a limiting of God within the limits of the creation, but a reverent looking to God as the one whose self-condescension is already [what constitutes] creation as creation."[71] That is, it is God's self-communication in and through the Word that establishes the true meaning of the created order.

While the perspectives we have just considered may indicate an affinity between the approaches of Barth and Pryzwara to analogical theology that is not immediately obvious, it would be wrong to overlook the substantial differences between them. The most important of these is as follows. An analogy of being is founded on the conviction that God's revelation in creation corresponds to and is fulfilled by God's revelation in the reconciliation of sinners by Christ. That is, if the knowledge of God that can be obtained by rational reflection on created being is to be true knowledge, it must not be in conflict with knowledge of God that comes through God's saving Word. Barth,

70. Betz, "Beyond the Sublime," 9–10.

71. Przywara, "Religionsphilosophie katholischer Theologie" cited in Betz, "Beyond the Sublime," 6–7.

however, cannot accept such a broad approach to revelation. The problem for Barth is that revelation through the creation relies upon the effective use of reason. But reason, while possessing a certain power, is ultimately defective as a result of the effects of sin. In order for God to break through the darkness that is in fallen human beings, God needed to speak a completely new Word—the Word of redemption in and through Christ. Revelation is nothing other than this new Word in Christ. Thus, any talk of being must be set in the context of divine redemption of human being.

The question of the relationship between *analogia entis* and *analogia fidei* is a complex one. In making the points that I have, the intention is not to attempt a settlement of all the major disputes. This is clearly beyond the scope of the present work. I have devoted space to this discussion because I see it as useful for identifying a number of principles that I take to be indispensable for any responsible analogical theology. These principles can be briefly stated as follows. First, the starting point in our knowledge of God is what God has revealed. Analogical theology is founded on the advent of God in Christ. Related to this is the principle that analogical theology generates true knowledge of God. An analogy of advent reveals God as the one who justifies sinful humanity in and through the death of Christ. Third, while analogical theology reveals similarity in the relation between humanity and God, it reveals an even greater dissimilarity. The profound otherness of God is acknowledged and respected in responsible analogical God-talk. The fourth principle is that primacy in the analogical relation is with God. That is, God has all the perfections perfectly and originally; we have them only imperfectly and derivatively. Finally, *analogia entis* and *analogia fidei* are not mutually exclusive options for analogical theology. I contend that these guidelines need to be adhered to in developing therapeutic analogues for preaching. More will be said on this below.

This last principle is not clearly articulated in the preceding discussion. It is, however, a very important one in the context of my approach to analogy and therapeutic preaching. It is therefore necessary to discuss more fully what is at stake. In his statements in the *Dogmatics*, I think that Barth overstates the case in relation to the failure of *analogia entis*. There, as we have seen, he avers that an analogy drawn from human experience can only hinder our efforts to know God. Barth contends that any human concept or experience that may on the surface seem to be analogous to something in God's being and nature is in the end so utterly different from it that it is of no use in knowing God. There is a chasm between the being of God and human being that is so vast that there is no way to build a bridge over it. It is certainly true, as I have already indicated, that all expressions of human ways-of-being are inevitably more dissimilar than similar to God's way-of-being. It is said that every analogy "limps." There is never a perfect correspondence between a thing and its analogue. In relation to analogical theology, the limp is an especially pronounced one because the finite is set as a likeness to the infinite. Nevertheless, analogues based on human nature and modes of being do have the capacity to throw some light on who God is. Reflection on human love, goodness, and wisdom does give us a glimpse—an important one, limited though it may be—of the being and nature of God. This is very significant in relation to my project. My approach to therapeutic preaching is grounded in the assumption that an analogous relation holds between the empathy, acceptance, and, where appropriate, confronting stance that a therapist expresses, on the one hand and the therapeutic nature of God on the other. If there is no place for an *analogia entis* in theology, my project fails. Having expressed the matter in this way, I need to make it clear that I am not thinking of "therapist" as an ontological category. Clearly it is not. The ontological category that applies here is human being. The essential nature of a human person—what she is *qua* human—is expressed very significantly, but not exclusively, through loving being-with. Therapists, when they are authentic, have a particular way of expressing love-in-relationship—namely, through stances such as acceptance and empathy, on the one hand and sensitive confrontation on the other.

The reason that I think that it is appropriate to do the kind of analogical work in a sermon that I am proposing is that I consider that a good case can be made that there is room for both *analogia fidei* and *analogia entis*. Even Barth finally came to this position, as we shall soon see.

Analogia fidei refers to "qualified words" that possess a likeness to the divine reality to which they point. But the interpretation of these words—words such as grace, redemption, and self-sacrifice—requires an *analogia entis*. As soon as a theologian begins to talk about God's saving action in Christ, she inevitably finds herself turning to analogies between God's way-of-being and human ways-of-being. A theologian will say, for example, grace is like the unconditional positive regard of a therapist or of any loving person (Tillich). Or she will suggest that the love of the cross is like the love of a mother, a lover, or a friend (McFague). Or the messianic feast celebrated by Jesus might be likened to the "open friendship" that all gracious persons offer (Moltmann). Barth himself drew an analogy between the love between the Father and the Son (actually the concrete situation of calling and being called), and that between a man and a woman: "It is not palpable that we have to do with a clear and simple correspondence, an *analogia relationis*, between this mark of the divine being, namely, that it includes an I and a Thou, and the being of man, male and female. The relationship between the summoning I in God's being and the summoned divine Thou is reflected both in the relationship of God to the man whom He has created, and also in the relationship between the I and the Thou, between male and female, in human existence itself."[72] Though at one point Barth was quick to point out that there is a clear distinction between his *analogia relationis* and the Catholic *analogia entis*, later he acknowledged that this did not altogether hold up (as we shall see below). What this demonstrates is that *analogia fidei* needs *analogia entis*. If one accepts this, the crucial issue in approaching the latter analogical strategy is the nature of the relationship between divine and human being. That is, we need to indicate where primacy should be assigned. The only theologically adequate response, the one that Aquinas advocated so strongly, is that primacy in the relation is with God. God gives archetypal expression to terms such as love, goodness, righteousness, wisdom, and redeemer; our expressions are ectypal. God's way of being loving, good, and righteous represents a perfect realization of these virtues. Human expressions are defective reproductions of the perfect original.

Despite his vigorous statement of his objections, Barth in the end opened up a place for *analogia entis* in theology. In *Church Dogmatics* II.1 §26, he discusses a pair of articles by the Romanic Catholic theologian Gottlieb Söhngen in which he, Söhngen, argues for "*analogia entis* within an *analogia fidei*." The Catholic theologian goes on to state that "the knowledge of the being of God is to be subordinated to the knowledge of the activity of God." Barth indicates his approval of this formula. He is prepared to welcome an *analogia entis* into the theological fold if, and only if, primacy is given to the analogy of faith. In answering a question after a lecture given at Princeton Theological Seminary in 1962, he elaborates on this position:

> Yes. Exactly speaking it is true that in the first volume of *Church Dogmatics* I said something very nasty about *analogia entis* . . . Later on I began to see that the notion of analogy cannot totally be suppressed by theology. I didn't at first speak of *analogia entis*. I spoke of an *analogia relationis* and then in a more biblical way of the analogy of faith. And then some of my critics said: "Well, after

72. Barth, *CD*, III.1, 196.

all, an *analogia relationis* is also some kind of *analogia entis.*" And
I couldn't completely deny it. I said: well, after all, if *analogia entis*
is interpreted as *analogia relationis* or analogy of faith, well, I will
no longer say nasty things about *analogia entis.*[73]

What is true for systematic theology is also true for the theology in the
therapeutic sermon. This latter theology needs to take its lead from *analogia
fidei*, but it may also incorporate *analogia entis.*

Analogy, Metaphor, and Therapeutic God-Talk in the Pulpit

The approach that I take in relation to the use in preaching of analogies drawn
from therapeutic discourse and practice accords with the Word theology
principle of the subordination of *analogia entis* to *analogia fidei.* The gospel is
not primarily about reason and knowledge of the being of God, though these
things are certainly implicated. It is primarily about the address of God to
humanity though Christ in the power of the Holy Spirit. The central event in
God's address to us is the word of the cross. It is this word that reveals God as
the God of all love, grace, and compassion. It is in God's nature and being to
reach out to suffering, confused, disoriented, and disordered humanity with
a word of love that heals and restores. This is the divine *therapeia.* It is an important dimension of the gospel (there are other equally important aspects)
and therefore of Christian proclamation. The analogues that are drawn from
therapeutic discourse and practice do not serve as the starting point for the
theological reflection on God's *therapeia* that takes place in sermon preparation and delivery. That is, the aim is not construed as using therapeutic
insights to develop some new knowledge of God's healing love. Rather, the
aim is to use insights from counseling theory and practice to find appropriate analogues that not only help to explain the nature of God's therapy as
expressed in the particular text, but that also facilitate greater openness to it.
That is, the analogues should not be seen as merely didactic aids. The goal
is not simply to provide some interesting insights. The analogues should be
seen first and foremost as instruments that serve to open the heart and mind
of the listener to God's healing grace. That is, they are used in an attempt
to strike a chord in the listener—to stimulate openness in faith to healing,
renewal, and transformation through divine *therapeia.*

---

73. Barth, "Gespräch in Princeton I" cited in Oakes, "The Question of Nature and
Grace," 605.

A second important principle in my approach to therapeutic God-talk in the pulpit is assigning primacy to God in the analogical relation between God and human experience. This is the point that Aquinas makes very strongly in his analogical theology. Though from a Word theology perspective, the starting point for theological reflection needs to be the gracious self-communication of God through Christ in the power of the Holy Spirit, Aquinas' approach does have something important to say to us. It is true that Thomas does suggest that reflection on human experience can lead to true knowledge of God. He identifies good effects in the human person—goodness, wisdom, etc.—and then attributes these by analogy to their source. Using this method, one can assign the names Goodness and Wisdom to God. But as we saw above, Aquinas considers that in this method primacy is not actually assigned to human being, but rather to divine being.[74] In a *metaphorical* way of speaking about God, on the other hand—in referring to God as king or as lion—the primacy is assigned to the creature. God is said to be like a particular creature. But in the case of analogy, the names that are used constitute the essence of God—God's essential nature is goodness and wisdom—and therefore the primacy is with God. Goodness and wisdom in the human person are only imperfectly realized; in God they are perfectly realized. This is because they only exist in humans because God has infused them into us. The only reality that is empirically observable is the human manifestation of these traits. Thus for Aquinas this is the only possible starting point for a scientific theology. However, this does not mean that primacy in relation to these traits is assigned to the human person. Goodness and wisdom are first in God and only secondarily in human beings.

What this observation means in practice is that the preacher of the therapeutic sermon needs to be careful lest she unwittingly fails to fully respect the majesty and glory of God. Analogical therapeutic preaching should not give the impression that God can be seen as fitting the mold of the psychotherapist. Theologically speaking, it is not that the empathy and acceptance of God are like that of a therapist; it is the other way around. The reason that an analogy can be drawn between God's way of being compassionate and psychotherapeutic compassion is that God is the condition of the possibility of all therapeutic healing.[75] God is the original therapist, so to speak; humans

---

74. See also on this Ricoeur, *The Rule of Metaphor*, 329.

75. Oden makes this point in *Kerygma and Counseling*, 21. He argues that there is a "tacit ontological assumption" in all psychotherapy. It is not just that the therapist accepts

participate in God's healing work. Using Aquinas' language, God is the cause of the effect that is empathy, or acceptance, or mirroring. It is in this sense that we talk about a mirroring God, an empathic God, etc.

A third principle in relation to the use of therapeutic God-talk in the pulpit is that such talk is properly analogical rather than metaphorical. A simple equation of metaphor and analogy is quite common in theological discourse. But as we saw above, there are good grounds for distinguishing the two. Analogy is mathematical in that it consists of a proportional equation: a:b::c:d. In a more general sense, we can say that analogy compares two things, which are alike in certain ways, in order to aid the explanation or clarification of some unfamiliar or difficult idea or object by showing how the idea or object is similar to a familiar one. We looked at many different theological analogues above. Science, of course, also needs analogues. Light is like a particle, and light is like a wave, for instance. The unfamiliar is light; the familiar is a particle/wave. Analogies are found—they either exist or do not exist. Metaphors, by contrast, are created. Let me offer an example of this—namely, the analogical form of the teleological argument (the argument for God's existence from design). The proponents of this argument contend that the existence of an Intelligent Designer can be deduced through establishing an analogy between the universe and machines. That is, it is stated that the universe (or at least parts of it) is like a machine. Machines have intelligent designers; a process of analogical reasoning leads to the truth that the universe must also have an intelligent designer. The argument uses a relatively and easily understandable thing—a machine— to understand a complex and difficult to understand thing—the universe. The teleological systems in the world that point to its machine-like quality mean that an appropriate analogy has been found. Either it is the case that the universe (or more properly, parts of it) is like a machine or it isn't. There is no logical opposition here. Metaphors, on the other hand, are created on the basis of creating a logical opposition that is not absurd. This argument is properly referred to as an analogical rather than a metaphorical approach because it is built on logic rather than distortion or twisting of meaning. Analogues are logical; metaphors are non-logical.

Another way of looking at this is to say that analogy has an explanatory function, whereas metaphor has a meaning-making function. We do

---

the client, but that the client is considered acceptable as a human being by the ground of being itself.

not want a twisting of logic in an analogy. The analogical relations must be clear for the analogy to serve its explanatory function.

Therapeutic metaphors for preaching such as the mirroring God and the empathic God simply represent attempts to articulate in a fresh way the primary metaphor, God is love. They are not used in the way that poetic metaphors are. The poet does not attempt to explicate her metaphors. The richness in a poetic metaphor comes from its superabundance of meaning. There is no fixed meaning for it. Even if the poet later writes a commentary and says, "When I used the metaphor 'virtue is the enamel on the soul' I meant x," x is not the full expression of it. A reader in possession of this knowledge need not feel totally constrained by it. She is quite at liberty to embrace an interpretation that she finds personally richer and more satisfying. The meaning in a poetic metaphor can be extended in many different directions. For this reason, a poet has no desire to close off options by including an analogy that makes her meaning clear: Enamel is to a material object as protection is to the soul.

What I am proposing is quite different to the way a poet operates. There is certainly value in introducing what the sermon is about through employing a therapeutically inspired metaphor. People are not used to putting God and mirrors or God and empathy together. Through the employment of semantic impertinence, the listener is engaged: "Now here's something I've not heard before. This might be worth tuning into." The major thrust of the kind of therapeutic sermon that I am proposing, however, is not the therapeutically inspired metaphor but rather the analogical theology that it is associated with. In her preparation, the preacher seeks to identify the way in which relevant counseling theory might be used to highlight the divine *therapeia* that is presented in the text. Not all texts, of course, will be amenable to this treatment. But if it looks like psychotherapeutic psychology may be a useful tool to use, she takes hold of it. What the preacher is trying to do in practical terms is to use an appropriate piece of counseling psychology to give a fresh articulation of the story of God's therapy that is told in the text. What she is doing theologically is to use an analogy to expose another facet of the diamond that is the comforting and confronting love of God. She is saying to the listener: "Here is a parallel from the world of counseling that may help you grasp a little more of the wonder, depth, and beauty of God's healing love that appears in our text." To use an example that we will discuss more fully in the next chapter, the acceptance the father communicates to the prodigal son in his warm embrace can be likened to the mirroring that psychotherapists do when they work with shame-prone persons. This, in turn, can be used to say something important about the character of God.

The work that we have been doing here on analogy and metaphor sets up important principles for the responsible use of counseling theory in the pulpit. These guidelines have been employed in developing the sermons presented in the final chapter.

6

Two Sermons with Commentary

I SAID ABOVE THAT divine *therapeia* consists of both comfort and help, on the one hand, and challenge and confrontation, on the other. God reaches out to us with compassion, empathy, and acceptance; but God also confronts our disordered, self-defeating, and destructive thinking and acting. The first sermon presented below features God's gracious acceptance of us in our shame and guilt. The shame experience of the prodigal son is highlighted, along with what I characterize as God's positive mirroring (acceptance, approval, and affirmation). The second sermon focuses on the problems of self-deception and disavowal of sub-selves that an individual finds threatening. In this way, a different light is cast on the familiar story of Jonah and the big fish. The way in which God confronts Jonah's disavowal of his egoism and exaggerated self-concern is explored.

"You Are Right, Good, Full of Quality"[1] (Luke 15:11–32)

The gospel passage from Luke that we have just heard read is a story of a loving father reaching out to his two sons. I want to focus on the experience of the younger of the two. I guess most people would say that there's not much to like about the prodigal son. He did some pretty despicable things. Let's draw up the list. Bad act no. 1: He treats his father as if he was dead. According to the laws of property, children were entitled to request a portion of the father's capital during his lifetime. But a son had the right

1. I am indebted to E. Moltmann-Wendell for this expression. See her "Self-love and Self-acceptance."

of disposal of the property only after the father's death. Bad act no. 2: The prodigal frittered away his means of caring for his father if the need arose. Bad act no. 3: He hooked up with a Gentile instead of going to the Jewish community for help. Bad act no. 4: By working with pigs, he chose to make his living in a sinful way. Not to put too fine a point on it, this lad is uncouth, unclean, and contemptible.

Some uncouth and contemptible people never change. They stay in the same pitiful rut. The prodigal decides it's time to get out of the rut. He composes a "sorry speech": "Father, I have sinned against heaven and before you; I am no longer worthy to be called your son; treat me as one of your hired servants." He may not be truly repentant, though. His main concern seems to be getting properly fed and housed. To achieve these aims, he needs to be reconciled to his father.

Right about now, you may be thinking something like this: "This is one of those sin, repentance, and forgiveness sermons." Those of us who have been around the church for a while have heard a lot about sin and guilt, and a lot about grace and forgiveness. It's our "bread and butter," so to speak. Well, maybe that's not the best way to talk about it. It makes it sound all very ordinary. But there's nothing ordinary about the grace of God in Christ.

This *is* a story about sin, guilt, and forgiveness. But there's something else in it. It's also about shame and acceptance. For quite a few years now, I have been making a study of shame and of how it can be healed. That has meant that I now see this very familiar story with fresh eyes. I can't help but see unmistakable indicators of the shame experience.

So what's shame all about? The first thing to say is that you can feel shame about almost anything. Some people condemn themselves as socially awkward, clumsy, and gauche. Others feel dull, incompetent, and ignorant. Cowardice and betrayal are especially potent sources of shame. It's possible to feel ashamed of one's appearance, height (or lack of it), weight, disability, or disfigurement. Shame can be associated with familial or national identity. In Middle Eastern societies, shame is the flip side of honor. Honor is a claim to worth and the social recognition of that worth. In such societies, there is an honor code. A person feels shame when she or he breaks the code. She or he experiences a loss of face.

Shame is about feeling inferior, inadequate, flawed. Shame-prone people don't think they are worth very much. There's an overlap with guilt, but there are also differences. I feel guilty over the bad things I've done, but I *am* my shame. The guilty person thinks, "I've done some bad things." The shame-prone person thinks, "*I'm* no good." In her mind, the problem is not what she has done but the self that she is. Her thoughts are shot through with self-loathing: "I'm stupid. I always mess things up. I'm a complete bore. I'm a loser."

Inferiority shame is linked to what a person sees as defects in her personality or her abilities—or in both these areas. If we're talking about inferiority shame, it's possible to make neat distinctions in relation to guilt. There's no guilt associated with having a dull personality. There's no guilt associated with having only moderate workplace skills. But when we get into the moral zone, shame and guilt can't be so cleanly separated out; they're tangled up together. I think that this is the case with the prodigal. He feels guilty about his moral transgressions, but he is also feeling a global sense of inferiority and worthlessness. When people talk about their shame they use images such as "dirty," "polluted," and "unclean." All three seem to fit in the case of this unfortunate young man. His self-esteem is almost nonexistent. The polite way in which a Middle Easterner got rid of a hanger-on was to give him a task that he knew would be refused. How could a self-respecting Jew take a job taking care of swine? This one did because he wasn't in fact self-respecting. The first words this lad will speak when he sees his father are, "I'm not worthy to be called your son."

Shame is all around us. Many people who suffer from it do not look dirty and unclean like the prodigal. But they do feel that way. I got quite a shock when I read an article written by an academic that I know and discovered that this is his story. Since it is in the public record, I'm free to recount it for you. In the times I've met Richard, I've found him to be confident, self-assured, and seemingly comfortable in his own skin. He's certainly good at what he does. While this is one side of Richard, there's another side that very few people see. This is the story that he tells in his article:

> Two years ago . . . I assisted, as a home hospice care volunteer, a person who was suffering from AIDS, who died during the last period of my care. After farewelling him and awaiting his end, I returned home, and woke up in the middle of the night in a state well described by [the psychotherapist] Kohut [when he talks about shame] . . . "empty, exhausted, drained, demoralized . . . deflated . . . passive, and weak." I cried inconsolably over this tragic loss, as I thought about him.
>
> [Richard goes on to say that the man who died was like a mirror for his own shame.] There is the self that had successfully done many useful things, and continues to do so, and the self

who for almost as long as I could remember continually told me, "You are shit."

When Richard says, "I think I'm a piece of crap," he isn't looking for forgiveness. What is he supposed to repent of? Is he supposed to say, "I'm sorry that I don't like myself very much"? When a person is feeling shame, what he or she is really looking for is acceptance and affirmation. The guilty person longs to hear, "You are forgiven." The shame-prone person aches for a loving, affirming embrace.

The father gives the son who was lost an embrace and a kiss. It's certainly true that there's some forgiving to be done. The son has seriously injured his dad. The kiss says, "I forgive you, son." But what stands out even more prominently for me is the healing of the son's shame. The way in which the father goes out to greet his son says a great deal. In the Middle Eastern culture, a man of his age was expected to maintain honor by walking at a dignified pace. To run as the father does means showing one's undergarments like a teenager. So great is his compassion, so great is his urgency to heal his son's shame, that he is prepared to bring shame upon himself.

There are some other really affirming actions performed by the father. The father calls for a robe. This is a symbol of honor. The shoes he calls for are a sign that he is a son and not a slave. The ring he places on his finger is an indication of authority. Think, lastly, about the party. The father doesn't plan a quiet family gathering. He makes a public gesture so that the whole community will know about his acceptance of this wayward son.

This is the most wonderful story of grace and acceptance shown by a truly extraordinary father. It's also a story about divine grace and acceptance. The height, length, and breadth of grace is too much for us to grasp. This story helps us get a handle on it. The grace of God is like that of this amazing man. The word "like" is important here. Human goodness can only ever be a pale reflection of divine goodness.

In thinking about the divine acceptance the parable points to, the image that came to my mind was the "mirroring God." Let me explain what I mean. In the extract from Richard's article that I read, he refers to Heinz Kohut. Kohut was a psychotherapist who worked extensively with shame-prone people. He found that the most effective way to help such people is to be consistently admiring, approving, and accepting. He called this "mirroring." The term is descriptive of what naturally takes place when loving parents interact with their young children. When the child reacts with delight over something good that she has done, the parents mirror her joy and excitement. Their faces light up in response to the child's beaming expression. The child sees her delight reflected on the faces of her parents. This dynamic is an important part of the process of building self-confidence and a sense of worth.

God's acceptance is like that of a mirroring therapist. But of course it's so much more. We can't fully grasp it; it's too much for us to take in. In thinking about mirroring, we catch a glimpse of it, and nothing more.

Even the most empathic and accepting therapist falls massively short of the wondrous gift that God offers us. Indeed, God is the ground of every compassionate and affirming act by a therapist. Every such act is a participation in divine love and acceptance. The power of God's love and grace makes mirroring possible—even when a therapist doesn't acknowledge God's presence.

The mirroring God says to us, "In my eyes, you are right, good, full of quality." It's not that we are so wonderful that God can't help but offer positive mirroring. Is the prodigal a wonderful person? We're talking about grace here. But we don't know how to talk about it, really. We don't have the words or the concepts to fully capture the nature of divine love and acceptance. So we tell a story of a father who rushes toward his wayward son to give him a kiss and a bear hug. Or we point to the child who is the gleam in her mother's eye. Most people at some point feel deep shame and guilt. Tragically, some of us are plagued by these feelings most of the time. But there is good news. The gospel offers hope, peace, and healing. The gospel offers a word of grace.

The word of grace is that faith in Christ and in the power of his death justifies us. Justification means that we have been put right with God. Christ's loving act heals both our guilt and our shame. Not only are we declared right with God, but we are also affirmed as good and full of quality. We say, "I am not worthy"; God says, "Let me take you in my arms." Take the word of grace to heart: "In my eyes, you are right, good, full of quality." Amen.

Commentary

A central aim in this sermon is to show that shame features along with guilt in the experience of the prodigal son. Over the past twenty years, there has been significant research conducted by pastoral theologians on shame and its healing.[2] In any discussion of shame, it is necessary to acknowledge

---

2. See, for example, Capps, *The Depleted Self*; Fowler, *Faithful Change*; Pembroke, *The Art of Listening*; Pattison, *Shame*; and Goodliff, *With Unveiled Face*.

that we are dealing not with a unitary concept but rather with a case of family resemblance. That is, there is significant variation in the way people experience shame. There are at least five members in the shame family—namely, situational shame, aesthetic shame, inherited identity shame, inferiority shame, and moral shame.[3] The term "situational shame" comes from Robert Karen.[4] It describes those embarrassing moments—slurping one's soup in polite company, tripping over one's shoelaces at an inopportune moment, a joke falling flat—which come to us all at some time. Clearly, we are dealing here with the low toxicity end of the shame spectrum.

Aesthetic shame is quite a bit more painful. In a culture which places such a high value on physical beauty, there is great potential for those who fall short of the ideal to feel shame. Whereas the ideal in other forms of shame may relate to intelligence, social skill, or moral strength, here we are dealing with an aesthetic ideal. When a person perceives a gap between her real self and her desired physical ideal, shame is the painful result.

Inherited identity shame is associated with the particular family, class, and culture a person is born into. Our inherited identity may be a source of pride. Sometimes, though, it carries with it a burden of shame.

The fourth member is inferiority shame. In broad terms, a sense of inferiority may be related either to talents and abilities or to personal qualities. A person may feel shame because she judges herself to be incompetent. That is, she is unhappy about the level of skill she has in certain key areas of her life. An individual may also feel shame because she considers that she is boring, timid, socially inept, lacks a sense of humor, to list just a few of the possibilities. Or she may feel ashamed on both counts.

The last member on our list is moral shame. Shame and pride both have a moral reference. Moral failure represents a transgression against the personal and social orders. Awareness of the harm that is done to these orders makes us ashamed. There is a strong argument that shame rather than guilt is the truly moral feeling. As Gary Thrane puts it, "Those who

3. Two leading shame researchers who have developed typologies are Robert Karen and James Fowler. The former suggests four categories, namely *existential shame* (the individual suddenly becomes aware of his failings), *class shame* (related to my category of *inherited identity shame*), *narcissistic shame* (one's personal identity is shame-based), and *situational shame* (a category I also use). See Karen, "Shame," 40–70, 58. Moving from "normal" shame to increasingly pathological variations, James Fowler describes five types and degrees. These are: *healthy shame, perfectionist shame, shame due to enforced minority shame* (cf. my *inherited identity shame*), *toxic shame* (cf. Karen's *narcissistic shame*), and *shamelessness*. See Fowler, *Faithful Change*, chap. 7.

4. Karen, "Shame," 58.

merely dread the punishing voice of conscience (guilt) are not moral. Only those who love their virtue and dread its loss (shame) are moral."[5] If the only motivation one has for moral behavior is the fear of guilty feelings, one's performance of good actions will be marred by the grudging spirit behind them. A person influenced by shame feelings, on the other hand, derives satisfaction from fulfilling her moral duty.

In the sermon, I make reference to the last two members on the list—namely, inferiority and moral shame. As far as we can tell from the evidence that we are given, the shame that the prodigal experiences is not related to either his personal incompetence or dissatisfaction with his personality. His emotional distress is not caused by perceived incompetence in certain key activities. Nor do we have any evidence that he is disgruntled with his personal makeup. His major problem is not that he thinks he is dull and uninteresting, for example. The primary source of his shame is his moral failure and the dishonoring of self and family that goes with it. He fails in a number of ways. He treats his father as if he is already dead. In squandering his property, he fails to make provision for the future care of his father. And he makes himself unclean by working with swine.

In the experience of moral shame, guilt also features. This is in contrast to inferiority shame. There is no guilt associated with cooking awful lasagna or with being clumsy in social situations!

It is common in the pastoral and psychological literature to distinguish between shame and guilt. Shame researchers consistently use the global aspect of the shame experience to differentiate it from its cousin in the affect family. A person feels guilty over actions (or omissions) that have caused harm to others. Guilt can be localized in a certain aspect of the self—namely, that which is associated with a particular moral transgression. A person who gambles excessively on occasion may say, "I like the person that I am. I just get carried away sometimes when I go down to the track." Shame, though, cannot be located in a discrete act that can be separated off from the self. The difference may be expressed this way: "I am guilty of this bad act; but I *am* my shame."

As Leon Wurmser observes, shame has a global quality because it is evoked by a discrepancy between a tested self and an ideal image.[6] This image is not simply constructed out of a delimited reality such as actions, but out of all the components that define a self. It is through shameful events that

5. Thrane, "Shame," 154.
6. Wurmser, "Shame," 86.

the self is revealed. Personal identity is shaped in this way. The shame events throw up the contours of a person's selfhood and of the world of reality she inhabits. Guilt may be assuaged by confession or restitution, but the experience of shame may be transcended only by a reshaping of identity.

With this in mind, I make the point in the sermon that the father offers both forgiveness and acceptance to his lost son. Acceptance is affirmation and approval of a person and of his or her basic identity. The father knows this son well. He knows all about his serious personal flaws and deficiencies. And yet he is prepared to run out and embrace him and then to throw a party for him. Through these actions, he welcomes back this deeply flawed son into the family and into the community. This is what a person experiencing deep shame desires most. He or she wants to be accepted in his or her weakness and deficiency. It is possible to reform morally wayward tendencies (as difficult as this may be); it is not possible to transform oneself into a completely new identity. The only hope for healing for a person plagued by shame is acceptance.

I am aware that some might object that in taking a largely psychological approach to the parable, I miss the fact that honor rather than self-esteem is the central value in the Middle Eastern culture. Honor is a claim to worth made by an individual that is recognized by the social group. It can either be acquired passively (by birth or inheritance) or actively (through excellence in fulfiling one's kinship and communal obligations and in meeting challenges from others). Dishonor, or shame, is the result of a loss of precedence or face. Since the time of Margaret Mead, there has been a tendency amongst anthropologists to contrast shame and guilt cultures. Shame is associated with small communities featuring face-to-face relations in which the disapproval of others is feared. Guilt is linked to Western, diversified, and industrialized societies and is said to result from an internal sanction related to a moral transgression. This neat distinction disregards, on the one hand, the fact that shame features in modern developed, socially differentiated, and anonymous societies (e.g., in the dock of a criminal court, in the tabloid press, and in public "naming and shaming" campaigns prosecuted by community leaders and lawmakers) and, on the other, that internalized sanctions against morally wrong actions feature in ancient cultures.[7] Peristiany and Pitt-Rivers clearly identify the problem with the old anthropological thesis:

7. See Cairns, "Representations of Remorse"; Siebert, *Construction of Shame*, 15–16; and Peristiany and Pitt-Rivers, "Introduction," 8.

> Those who exemplified guilt culture were . . . by implication sup-
> porters of the definition of honor which derived it from virtue, those
> of shame culture took a view somewhat closer to that of Hobbes and
> interpreted it as above all a matter of precedence. Guilt related to
> lack of virtue, shame to the loss of precedence or face. In fact, both
> approaches appear to be necessary, and in a sense complementary,
> since the function of the concept of honor is precisely . . . to equate
> them and establish thereby the dialectic between . . . "the world as
> it ought to be and the world as it is." But the idea of reifying the dis-
> tinction between guilt and shame and attaching it specifically to one
> culture or another removed the possibility of understanding either,
> since the first essential step in such an endeavor is to examine their
> coexistence within a single culture.[8]

In a culture in which honor is the primary value and shame is the major source of distress, individuals are not bereft of a moral conscience. They feel the weight of internal sanctions when they fall into moral transgression. The situation that Peristiany and Pitt-Rivers describe fits perfectly, of course, with that of Israel and of the earliest Christian community. The shame of losing face and the guilt associated with transgression of divine law both featured in these communities. Both these dynamics can be clearly seen in the parable. The prodigal says to his father, "I have sinned against heaven and before you." He is guilty of sin. In the sermon, I complicate things by showing that guilt and shame are tied up together in the prodigal's experience. It is also the case, further, that the sins of the prodigal represent a breach of the honor code. Through treating his father and the Jewish community so disrespectfully, he dishonors both himself and his family. The father wishes to spare him the shaming stares of the villagers, so he runs to the outskirts to greet him. The fact that the old man runs constitutes a loss of face. The robe, the shoes, and the ring, finally, have to do with conferring honor and status.

Though I refer to the honor/shame dialectic and to its prominence in Middle Eastern societies, I take a largely psychological approach in the sermon. I come to it with the thinking about shame and guilt that comes from psychotherapeutic experience. Though some may want to raise the objection that this constitutes a reading of twenty-first century Western interests and concerns into a first century Middle Eastern context, there is a good argument to be made that in both contexts the emotional side of shame is a factor. The sociologist, Thomas Scheff, begins his analysis by pointing out

8. Peristiany and Pitt-Rivers, "Introduction," 8.

that shame is a social phenomenon; it is associated with societal norms and sanctions. But he also draws attention to the emotional component in the system.[9] There are the rewarding emotions of pride and fellow feeling, on the one hand, and the punishing emotions of embarrassment, shame, and humiliation, on the other. This emotional side of the experience of shame is relevant whether we are talking about a modern culture or an ancient one. It is therefore not out of place to bring a predominantly psychological perspective to the experience of the prodigal.

In the chapter on correlation (chapter 4), I indicated that there is a danger associated with approaching a text with a psychological theory in hand. It is very easy to fall into the trap of manipulating the biblical story to fit that theory. It is not possible to find in any biblical text the clear signs of a particular form of emotional distress that one would find in the transcripts from a series of counseling sessions. It is therefore a matter of judgment as to whether or not it is legitimate to identify shame as a major source of distress for the prodigal. In my estimation, the actions and circumstances described in the story, combined with the fact that the prodigal says to his father, "I am no longer worthy to be called your son," represent a strong indication that this is the case. At the core of the shame experience is the soul-destroying feeling of unworthiness. It is the feeling of not being good enough, of being unacceptable, of being an outcast. The other clear indication for me is that shame-prone people use images such as "dirty," "polluted," and "unclean" to describe their experience. These terms seem to fit particularly well with the state that the prodigal has fallen into.

Use is made in the sermon of metaphors and analogues informed by therapeutic concepts. In chapter 5 where these matters were discussed, reference was made to Aquinas' principle that primacy should be assigned to God in the analogical relation between God and human experience. In recognition of this, I make the statement in the sermon that God is the condition of the possibility of all psychological healing.

Also in that chapter, I noted the theological principle that in any analogical relationship one constructs between God and humanity, the dissimilarity is far greater than the similarity. With this in mind, I declare that: "Even the most empathic and accepting therapist falls massively short of the wondrous gift that God offers us."

The last point that I want to raise has to do with the theocentric focus in the model of therapeutic preaching that I have developed. Some may

9. See Scheff, *Microsociology*, 73–77.

wonder how this principle is embodied in the sermon when so much attention is given to human agents and to shame theory. Even though the amount of space allotted to each category may seem to suggest otherwise, I have endeavored to be faithful to the principle articulated in chapter 1— namely, that *therapeia* is the servant of *kerygma*. What primarily motivates me in this sermon is the proclamation of the grace of God in Christ. It is the grace that is manifested in God's declaration to those who put their trust in Christ: "In my eyes, you are right, good, full of quality." The information that is provided on shame and on its healing through mirroring is included not so much for its own sake. It is certainly helpful psychological information and may produce real insight in some of the listeners. But the main motivation behind the inclusion of this material is to highlight the divine grace that this story so beautifully points to.

"God's Therapy for Jonah" (Jonah 3:1–5, 10; 4:1–10)

How do you think about the self, about the self that you are? You will be aware of a center of initiative within you that drives your thinking, willing, feeling, and acting. There's a unified entity that we call the self. But if you think about it for a moment, there's also multiplicity in the self that you are. We often hear people make a comment along the lines, "I've got an aggressive side that comes out some times." Or, "I'm quite a shy person in one-to-one interactions, but strangely enough I'm quite comfortable speaking in front of a crowd." Or, to give one last example, a person may say, "I'm usually not particular fussy, but when it comes to my piano playing, I have to get it just right." We could say that there is within each of us a community of selves. The community of a particular individual might be made up of a loving self, an aggressive self, an anxious self, a competitive self, a parental self, a romantic self, an intellectual self, a responsible self, and a fun-loving self.

All of us, to a greater or lesser extent, experience trouble in the community of the self. There are those selves that we like, that make us feel good about ourselves. But there are others that we are not so sure about. In fact, some of them we dislike quite intensely. These selves tend to get disowned. We don't want to recognize them as belonging to us; they get pushed out of consciousness. I recently came across a report of a pastoral encounter that beautifully illustrates this common trap. "Mike" asked to see his pastor, "Jenny," because at the time he was experiencing difficulties in his professional relationships with some of his colleagues in the sociology department where he is a lecturer. Mike is thirty-four and is a gentle-natured, sensitive, and affable person who highly values harmonious relationships. He works hard at being flexible and accommodating in order to get on with his colleagues. However, Mike feels that his position is often not listened to and that others just push their ideas through "like a steam roller." After a meeting in which he feels that these dynamics have been in play, Mike often lies awake all night "stewing."

In one of their conversations, Jenny reflected with Mike on what happened at a recent meeting. I've asked Lesley to read the part of Jenny and Ralph to take the part of Mike. Thanks guys.

> J: How was yesterday's departmental meeting, Mike?
>
> M: Yeah, not too bad, as meetings go. But there were a couple of things I wasn't happy about.
>
> J: Such as?
>
> M: Well, for one Tom Jackson is all fired up about developing online courses, and the other staff members were pretty positive about it. But I'm not so sure. I feel quite strongly that personal contact with lecturers is a very important part of the student experience.
>
> J: Did you feel like the others heard you?
>
> M: Oh, I didn't say too much. I could see that things might get a bit heated.

As Jenny and Mike met over the ensuing weeks, Jenny noticed a pattern emerging. Mike is very mild and understated in his contributions even when he feels strongly about something. He then rationalizes his soft approach with statements such as, "It wasn't really a big deal anyway" or "It wasn't worth an argument" or "I really hate to hurt a person's feelings." When a variant of this pattern presented itself in one of their conversations, Jenny sensed that what might be most helpful to Mike would be to gently lift the lid on the cover story he is running. It's over to you again, Lesley and Ralph.

> M: I probably could have been a bit more forthright, but I was afraid that Sarah [one of Mike's colleagues] would be really hurt if I did.
>
> J: Mike, I really appreciate your sensitivity in the way you relate to others. I'm wondering, though, if behind your "softly, softly" approach there are actually two things going on. The first thing you are very happy to own. You value harmonious relationships and you work hard at being flexible and sensitive to the feelings of others. But I think that there may be something else

going on that you don't want to acknowledge. It has to do with a side of yourself that you don't like very much. Could it be that part of the reason that you don't say your piece is that you really need to please others and the thought that someone might be angry and disappointed with you is real scary for you?

M: So you think I'm a wimp? Is that it?

J: No I don't think that you're a wimp. You are a kind, sensitive, lovely man. But I do think that you have an inordinate fear of disapproval from others. It would help you if you could come to grips with that.

M: I don't know what to say . . . It's good to be gentle and loving. Isn't that the way Christians are supposed to be?

J: Gentle and loving, yes, but we should also feel free to say something that we believe in even if it makes others uncomfortable or even angry.

M: Look, the reason that the meetings are often so awful is that everyone feels *too* free to say their piece. It would be a heck of a lot better if people just thought a *tiny* bit more about the feelings of others! But no, everyone just wants to push their ideas through. I'm not the problem in all this!

J: Maybe you're hearing what I said as a personal attack; it certainly wasn't meant to be.

M: Look, this is really hard. I think that I just need some time to process what you've said.

J: Of course. Let's leave it for today and we can talk again when you are ready.

Do you see what is going on here? Everybody likes to be liked. Counselors are no different. This is not an easy step for Jenny to take. She loves Mike enough to be really honest with him. She loves him enough to confront him—to confront him in a sensitive and respectful way, that is.

What I find so interesting about God's dealings with Jonah is that something very similar is going on. Jonah, like Mike, is running a cover story. On the surface, it might seem that Jonah is expressing righteous anger. That is, he is feeling anger against God because God has failed to honor his own system of justice. But what Jonah is hiding from himself is his egoism and exaggerated self-concern. God is on to him, though. God knows all about Jonah's self-deception and he's not going to let him get away with it. There is real subtlety in the way God deals with the wayward prophet.

God doesn't confront him head-on, but instead plays a game with him. It's a serious game, of course. Its purpose is to lift the lid on Jonah's cover story.

The story of Jonah begins with God commanding the prophet to go at once to the capital of the great Assyrian empire to speak out against the wickedness of the people. But Jonah didn't like that idea too much and decided to flee to Tarshish instead. Why was Jonah so unwilling to carry out the Lord's commission to go to Nineveh and call the citizens to repentance? There are a number of possibilities that we could think of. Perhaps it was fear that was behind Jonah's flight toward Tarshish. It could also be that if Jonah prophesied against Nineveh and it wasn't destroyed, then Jonah would be made to look like a false prophet. Another good possibility is that Jonah's flight was motivated by a desire to protect Israel and his own reputation. He suspected Nineveh might repent and God would relent. Then the Lord would be angry with Israel for itself being so slow to repent and Jonah, who had announced impending doom for Nineveh, would be seen as a lying prophet.

These are all good guesses. But I want to suggest that the flight, his tumbling about in the ship on the wild seas, the encounter with the big fish, and everything we heard about in today's reading are all part of God's game strategy. The focus for this playful dialogue is Jonah's anger. On the surface, it may seem that the prophet is angry because he is distressed that God failed to honor the demands of his own system of justice. Jonah upholds the ancient tradition that sin must be punished; there should be no relenting on God's part. I think, though, that Jonah is kidding himself. He's happy with the thought that he's gripped by righteous anger. That makes him feel quite noble. What he is running from in the process is his self-assertion and egoism. Focusing on what he sees as God's failure keeps his own issues at arm's length.

So why does Jonah feel entitled to self-pity? Jonah subscribes to a view that when a message of God is authentically received and faithfully proclaimed it is bound to be fulfilled. The corollary is that if such a message is not fulfilled the reputation of the prophet is destroyed. It's the fact that God, through his act of mercy, has allowed him—Jonah—to fall into disrepute that causes Jonah to be enraged.

Recall how chapter 4 opens:

> But Jonah was greatly displeased and became angry. He prayed to the Lord, "O Lord, is this not what I said when I was still at home? That is why I was so quick to flee to Tarshish. I knew that you are a gracious and compassionate God, slow to anger and abounding in

love, a God who relents from sending calamity. Now, O Lord, take away my life, for it is better for me to die than to live."

Jonah's uses what looks like a celebration of God's grace and mercy as a reproach against God. The prophet wants to cast his anger in terms of theodicy. He is asking God to justify his decision to have mercy on the merciless Ninevites. I think that this is really a cover story. What Jonah is hiding from himself is his own egoism and exaggerated self-concern. He avows his righteous anger; he disavows his own egoism and self-pity.

God can see through the cover story, though, and he means to do something about it. God's approach is a subtle one. He does not directly confront Jonah over his self-deception. The Lord does not say, for instance, "You think you can convince me that you are concerned about divine justice, but I can see that the real issue is your arrogance and egoism." Instead God begins a game with the prophet. He asks: "Have you any right to be angry?" God begins to nudge Jonah toward self-examination.

Jonah, not surprisingly, forcefully resists God's lead. He heads off to the east of the city and builds himself a shelter as he waits to see if there will be a reversal. Perhaps, he muses, the Ninevites will relapse and God will punish them as they deserve. This wordless response is his defiant reply. His self-concern and arrogance are displayed in the way he directs his focus away from God's question and onto the fate of the city.

God continues his game as he provides a plant for shelter from the burning sun. When he sends a worm to eat it and a hot east wind to heighten the effects of the loss of shelter, Jonah's cover story is all but in tatters. His death wish says it all. Earlier Jonah was indignant because God took pity on Nineveh. Now it is self-pity that sparks his indignation. The fact that Jonah is ready to die because there is no more shade says something. It tells us how deeply mired in self-pity he is. It exposes the fact that his first expression of unwillingness to go to Nineveh was also deeply rooted in self-pity, not in genuine concern about the validity of God's justice.

God, meanwhile, is patient and continues to push the prophet to honest self-reflection. He asks, "Do you have a right to be angry about the vine?" God still has the hope that Jonah will reclaim the egoistic self he has isolated and is refusing to take responsibility for. In the end, Jonah fails to reach that point. We are left with God contrasting Jonah's compassion for the plant with his own compassion for the city.

Helping a person see what he desperately does not want to see is no easy task, not even for Almighty God! God calls us to conform ourselves ever more closely to the way of Christ. Let's have the courage to honestly look inside ourselves. What members of the community that is the self are taking us away from Christ? What are the sub-selves that we desperately don't want to acknowledge? What is God saying to us about the need for reform? What is the cover story that we are running that God is seeking to blow open? Today we have heard a call to be honest, to find the courage to face ourselves as we truly are, to open ourselves to the love and wisdom of God. May we, with the grace of God, find a way to heed that call. Amen.

Commentary

Contemporary psychologists typically talk about the self in terms of both multiplicity and unity. There is a unifying center of initiative that we call the self; but there is also a system of sub-selves. But this is not something new; Freud, Jung, and Berne had the same idea. The id may be construed as a metaphor for an instinctual self (itself composed of a sexual self and an aggressive self); the ego as symbolizing an executive self; and the superego as representing a moralizing/civilizing self.

Jung refers to the ego, Self, anima/animus, the persona, and the shadow. All of these can be thought of as sub-selves.

The P-A-C conceptualization of the self that Eric Berne developed likewise contains a reference to sub-selves. Persons grow up under the influence of a whole host of parental injunctions, rules, values, and taboos. They carry a "Parent-self" around inside them. They also live with a "Child-self." Dysfunctional emotional reactions developed in childhood break out in current stressful situations. The "Adult-self," lastly, represents the rational faculty which is able to challenge parental injunctions and modify dysfunctional emotional patterns.

The British psychotherapist, John Rowan, has perhaps done the most to build our understanding of the communitarian nature of the self. He was led to think about sub-selves—he uses the term "subpersonalities"—through his personal experience.[10] Through Gestalt therapeutic work he found himself discovering various "aspects" of his personality. Later, he began to realize that these aspects could be grouped together to form subpersonalities. He defines a subpersonality as "a semi-permanent and semi-autonomous region of the personality capable of acting as a person."[11]

10. Rowan, *Subpersonalities*, 46ff.
11. Ibid., 8.

The American psychologists, Hazel Markus and Paula Nurius, situate the community of the self in the context of the future.[12] They talk about the selves we can become and they call these "possible selves." Possible selves refer to how we imaginatively construct our future existence. Caught up in a vision of potential selves are a person's hopes and dreams, along with her fears and anxieties. A possible self is the ideal self a person dreams of. But it can also be a self she is afraid of becoming. "The possible selves that are hoped for might include the successful self, the creative self, the rich self, the thin self, or the loved and admired self, whereas the dreaded possible selves could be the alone self, the depressed self, the incompetent self, the alcoholic self, the unemployed self, or the bag lady self."[13]

This psychological theory about the self and its sub-selves sits behind the opening to the sermon. The scene is set for my interpretation of the Jonah story through reference to our tendency to own certain selves and to disown others. I see in Jonah avowal of his righteous anger and disavowal of his self-assertion and exaggerated self-concern. He accepts the self that upholds the ancient view of divine justice; he refuses to accept that he has a strong egoistic self.

I first started thinking about the encounter between God and Jonah in terms of a confrontation over a disavowed self in the course of writing my first book, *The Art of Listening*. I came across a commentary by H. W. Wolff[14] that helped me see the novella in an entirely different light. Wolff's approach is quite different to the conventional ones. In his commentary, James Limburg outlines traditional answers to the question of Jonah's resistance to the divine call.[15] Josephus suggests that it was fear that was behind Jonah's flight towards Tarshish. In the first-century CE book, *Lives of the Prophets*, the suggestion is made that if Jonah prophesied against Nineveh and it was not destroyed, then Jonah would be made to look like a false prophet. The ninth-century CE work, *Pirke de Rabbi Eliezer*, offers the view that motivating Jonah's flight was a desire to protect Israel and his own reputation. He suspected Nineveh might repent and God would relent. Then the Lord would be angry with his chosen people for being so slow to repent and Jonah, who had announced impending doom for Nineveh, would be seen as a lying prophet.

12. Markus and Nurius, "Possible Selves."

13 Ibid., 954.

14. Wolff, *Obadiah and Jonah*, 169.

15. Limburg, *Jonah*, 42–43.

The answer to the question of why Jonah took flight becomes clear in the dialogue between God and Jonah in chapter 4. Wolff describes this interplay between the two as playful: "The Creator of all things begins a game with him, just as Wisdom, God's delight, plays a game before the Creator on the inhabited globe . . . Just as in 1:17 God 'appointed' the great fish . . . so he now appoints a castor oil plant."[16] The focus for this playful dialogue is Jonah's anger. On the surface, it may seem that the prophet is angry because he is distressed that God failed to honor the demands of his own system of justice. Jonah upholds the ancient tradition that sin must be punished; there should be no relenting on God's part. Certainly a number of interpreters take this line.[17] I contend, though, following Wolff, that the real concern is not theodicy but Jonah's self-assertion.[18] In the sermon, I follow Wolff's line that God engages in a playful dialogue aimed at leading the wayward prophet to acknowledge his egoism and exaggerated self-concern.

16. Wolff, *Obadiah and* Jonah, 169.

17. Salters provides a convenient summary of such views. See his *Jonah and Lamentations*, 56–57.

18. Wolff, *Obadiah and Jonah*, 176.

Bibliography

Allen, Ronald J. "Preaching as Mutual Critical Correlation through Conversation." In *Purposes of Preaching*, edited by Jana Childers, 1–22. St. Louis: Chalice, 2004.

Aquinas, Thomas. *On the Truth of the Catholic Faith: Summa Contra Gentiles: Book One: God*. Translated by Anton C. Pegis. Garden City: Doubleday, 1955.

———. *The Treatise on the Divine Nature: Summa Theologiae I 1–13*. Translated by Brian J. Shanley. Indianapolis: Hackett, 2006.

Aristotle. *Poetics*. Translated by Samuel H. Butcher. New York: Hill & Wang, 1961.

Austin, John L. *How to Do Things with Words*. Oxford: Clarendon, 1962.

Barth, Karl. *Church Dogmatics*. Vol. 1, pt. 1. The Digital Karl Barth Library. Alexander Street Press, 2013. http://solomon.dkbl.alexanderstreet.com/.

———. *Church Dogmatics*. Vol. 2, pt. 1. The Digital Karl Barth Library. Alexander Street Press, 2013. http://solomon.dkbl.alexanderstreet.com/.

———. *The Early Preaching of Karl Barth: Fourteen Sermons With Commentary by William H. Willimon*. With William H. Willimon. Translated by John E. Wilson. Louisville: Westminster John Knox, 2009.

———. *Homiletics*. Translated by Geoffrey W. Bromiley and Donald E. Daniels. Louisville: Westminster John Knox, 1991.

———. *The Word of God and the Word of Man*. London: Hodder & Stoughton, 1928.

Beardsley, Monroe C. "The Metaphorical Twist." *Philosophy and Phenomenological Research* 22 (1962) 293–307.

Beggiani, Seely J. "Theology at the Service of Mysticism." *Theological Studies* 57 (1996) 201–33.

Betz, John R. "Beyond the Sublime: The Aesthetics of the Analogy of Being (Part 2)." *Modern Theology* 2 (2006) 1–50.

Black, Max. *Models and Metaphors*. Ithaca, NY: Cornell University Press, 1962.

Bultmann, Rudolph. "New Testament and Mythology: The Problem of Demythologizing the New Testament Proclamation." In *New Testament and Mythology and Other Basic Writings*, edited and translated by Shubert M. Ogden, 1–43. Philadelphia: Fortress, 1984.

———. "On the Problem of Demythologizing." In *New Testament and Mythology and Other Basic Writings*, edited and translated by Shubert M. Ogden, 95–130. Philadelphia: Fortress, 1984.

———. "Preaching: Genuine and Secularized." In *Religion and Culture: Essays in Honor of Paul Tillich*, edited by Walter Leibrecht, 236–42. London: SCM, 1958.

Buttrick, David. "Preaching in an *Un*brave New World." *The Spire* 13 (1988) 12.

Cairns, Douglas. "Representations of Remorse and Reparation in Classical Greece." In *Remorse and Reparation*, edited by Murray Cox, 171–78. London: Jessica Kingsley, 1999.

Campbell, Charles. *Preaching Jesus: The New Directions for Homiletics in Hans Frei's Postliberal Theology*. Eugene, OR: Wipf & Stock, 2006.

Capps, Donald. *The Depleted Self: Sin in a Narcissistic Age*. Minneapolis: Fortress, 1993.

———. *Pastoral Counseling and Preaching: A Quest for an Integrated Ministry*. Philadelphia: Westminster, 1980.

Clayton, John P. *The Concept of Correlation: Paul Tillich and the Possibility of a Mediating Theology*. Berlin: Walter de Gruyter, 1980.

Clements, Keith. *Friedrich Schleiermacher: Pioneer of Modern Theology*. London: Collins, 1987.

Corrigan, Kevin, and L. Michael. "Pseudo-Dionysius the Areopagite." The Stanford Encyclopedia of Philosophy. February 1, 2011. Online: http://plato.stanford.edu/archives/spr2011/entries/pseudo-dionysius-areopagite/.

Craddock, Fred. *As One without Authority*. 4th ed. St. Louis: Chalice, 2001.

———. "Preaching: An Appeal to Memory." In *What's the Matter with Preaching Today?*, edited by Mike Graves, 59–73. Louisville: Westminster John Knox, 2004.

DeHart, Paul. "On Being Heard but Not Seen: Milbank and Lash on Aquinas, Analogy, and Agnosticism." *Modern Theology* 26 (2010) 243–77.

Ebeling, Gerhard. *Theology and Proclamation: A Discussion with Rudolf Bultmann*. Translated by John Riches. London: Collins, 1966.

———. "Word of God and Hermeneutic." In *The New Hermeneutic*, edited by James M. Robinson and John B. Cobb, 78–110. New York: Harper & Row, 1964.

Ellingsen, Mark. *The Integrity of Biblical Narrative: Story in Theology and Proclamation* Eugene, OR: Wipf & Stock, 2002.

Fosdick, Harry E. *The Living of These Days: An Autobiography*. New York: Harper, 1956.

———. *Living Under Tension*. New York: Harper, 1941.

———. "Personal Counseling and Preaching." *Pastoral Psychology* 3 (1952) 11–15.

———. "What is the Matter with Preaching?" In *What's the Matter with Preaching Today?*, edited by Mike Graves, 7–19. Louisville: Westminster John Knox, 2004.

Fowler, James. *Faithful Change: The Personal and Public Challenges of Postmodern Life* Nashville: Abingdon, 1996.

Frei, Hans. *The Eclipse of Biblical Narrative*. New Haven, CT: Yale University Press, 1974.

———. *The Identity of Jesus: The Hermeneutical Bases of Dogmatic Theology*. Philadelphia: Fortress, 1975.

Fuchs, Ernst. "The New Testament and the Hermeneutical Problem." In *The New Hermeneutic*, edited by James M. Robinson and John B. Cobb, 111–45. New York: Harper & Row, 1964.

———. "Proclamation and Speech-Event." *Theology Today* 19 (1962) 341–54.

Gerhart, Mary, and Allan M. Russell. *Metaphoric Process: The Creation of Scientific and Religious Understanding*. Fort Worth: Texas Christian University Press, 1984.

Goodliff, Paul. *With Unveiled Face: A Pastoral and Theological Exploration of Shame* London: Darton, Longman & Todd, 2005.

Graham, Elaine, et al. *Theological Reflection: Methods*. London: SCM, 2005.

Graves, Mike. "God of Grace and Glory." In *What's the Matter with Preaching Today?*, edited by Mike Graves, 109–25. Louisville: Westminster John Knox, 2004.

Hammond, Guyton B. "An Examination of Tillich's Method of Correlation." *Journal of Bible and Religion* 32 (1964) 248–51.

Harrison, Peter. "Correlation and Theology: Barth and Tillich Re-Examined." *Studies in Religion/Sciences Religieuses* 15 (1986) 65–76.

Hiltner, Seward. *Preface to Pastoral Theology*. Nashville: Abingdon, 1958.

Immink, F. Gerrit. *Faith: A Practical Theological Reconstruction*. Translated by Reinder Bruinsma. Grand Rapids: Eerdmans, 2005.

Jackson, Edgar N. *How to Preach to People's Needs*. Nashville: Abingdon, 1956.

Johnson, Keith L. "Reconsidering Barth's Rejection of Pryzwara's *Analogia Entis*." *Modern Theology* 26 (2010) 633–50.

Jüngel, Eberhard. *God as the Mystery of the World*. Translated by Darrell L. Guder. Grand Rapids: Eerdmans, 1983.

Kant, Immanuel. *Prolegomena to Any Future Metaphysics*. New York: Liberal Arts Press, 1950.

Karen, Robert. "Shame." *Atlantic Monthly*, February 1992, 40–70.

Kay, James. *Preaching and Theology*. St. Louis: Chalice, 2007.

Kellenberger, James. "The Slippery Slope of Religious Relativism." *Religious Studies* 21 (1985) 39–52.

Lakoff, George, and Mark Johnson. *Metaphors We Live By*. Chicago: University of Chicago Press, 1980.

Lash, Nicholas. "Ideology, Metaphor and Analogy." In *Theology on the Way to Emmaus*, 95–119. London: SCM, 1986.

Limburg, James. *Jonah: A Commentary*. London: SCM, 1993.

Linn, Edmund H. *Preaching as Counseling: The Unique Method of Harry Emerson Fosdick*. Valley Forge, PA: Judson, 1966.

Long, Thomas G. "No News is Bad News." In *What's the Matter with Preaching Today?*, edited by Mike Graves, 145–57. Louisville: Westminster John Knox, 2004.

Lowry, Eugene L. *Doing Time in the Pulpit: The Relationship between Narrative and Preaching*. Nashville: Abingdon, 1985.

Markus, Hazel, and Paula Nurius. "Possible Selves." *American Psychologist* 41 (1986) 954–69.

Maximus Confessor. *Maximus Confessor: Selected Writings*. Translated by George C. Berthold. London: SPCK, 1985.

McCool, Gerald. Introduction to "Relationship between Nature and Grace: The Supernatural Existential." In *A Rahner Reader*, edited by Gerald McCool, 185. London: Darton, Longman, and Todd, 1975.

McFague, Sallie. *Metaphorical Theology: Models of God in Religious Language*. Philadelphia: Fortress, 1982.

———. *Models of God: Theology for an Ecological, Nuclear Age*. Philadelphia: Fortress, 1987.

Miller, Robert M. *Harry Emerson Fosdick: Preacher, Pastor, Prophet*. Oxford: Oxford University Press, 1985.

Moltmann-Wendell, Elizabeth. "Self-Love and Self-Acceptance." *Pacifica* 5 (1992) 288–301.

Nichols, J. Randall. *The Restoring Word: Preaching as Pastoral Communication*. San Francisco: Harper & Row, 1987.

Northcutt, Kay B. *Kindling Desire for God: Preaching as Spiritual Direction*. Minneapolis: Fortress, 2009.

Nouwen, Henri, *Creative Ministry*. New York: Doubleday, 1971.

Oakes, Kenneth. "The Question of Nature and Grace in Karl Barth: Humanity as Creature and as Covenant-Partner." *Modern Theology* 23 (2007) 595–616.

Oden, Thomas C. *Kerygma and Counseling*. Philadelphia: Westminster, 1966.

Pattison, Stephen. *Shame: Theory, Therapy, Theology*. Cambridge: Cambridge University Press, 2000.

Pembroke, Neil. *The Art of Listening: Dialogue, Shame, and Pastoral Care*. Grand Rapids: Eerdmans, 2002.

Peristiany, J. G., and Julian Pitt-Rivers. "Introduction." In *Honor and Grace in Anthropology*, edited by J. G. Peristiany and Julian Pitt-Rivers, 1–18. Cambridge: Cambridge University Press, 2005.

Pseudo-Dionysius, the Areopagite. *On the Divine Names and the Mystical Theology*. Translated by Clarence E. Rolt. London: SPCK, 1940.

Rahner, Karl. "Anonymous and Explicit Faith." In *Theological Investigations*, 16:52–59. London: Darton, Longman, and Todd, 1979.

———. *Meditations on Freedom and the Spirit*. London: Burns and Oates, 1977.

Ramsey, G. Lee. *Care-full Preaching: From Sermon to Caring Community*. St. Louis: Chalice, 2000.

Richards, Ivor A. *The Philosophy of Rhetoric*. London: Oxford University Press, 1936.

Ricoeur, Paul. *The Rule of Metaphor: Multi-Disciplinary Studies of the Creation of Meaning in Language*. Translated by Robert Czerny. London: Routledge, 2003.

Rorem, Paul. "Negative Theologies and the Cross." *Harvard Theological Review* 101 (2008) 451–62.

Rowan, John. *Subpersonalities: The People Inside Us*. London: Routledge, 1990.

Salters, Robin B. *Jonah and Lamentations*. Sheffield, UK: Sheffield Academic Press, 1994.

Scheff, Thomas J. *Microsociology: Discourse, Emotion, and Social Structure*. Chicago: University of Chicago Press, 1990.

Schleiermacher, Friedrich. *The Christian Faith*. Translated by Hugh R. Macintosh and James S. Stewart. Philadelphia: Fortress, 1976.

———. *On Religion: Speeches to its Cultured Despisers*. Translated by Richard Crouter. Cambridge: Cambridge University Press, 1988.

Siebert, Johanna. *The Construction of Shame in the Hebrew Bible: The Prophetic Contribution*. London: Sheffield Academic Press, 2002.

Sphar, Asa A., III, and Argile R. Smith. *Helping Hurting People: A Handbook of Reconciliation-Focused Counseling and Preaching*. Lanham, MD: University of America Press, 2002.

Switzer, David. *Pastor, Preacher, Person: Developing a Pastoral Ministry in Depth*. Nashville: Abingdon, 1979.

Teikmanis, Arthur L. *Preaching and Pastoral Care*. Englewood Cliffs. NJ: Prentice-Hall, 1964.

Thrane, Gary. "Shame." *Journal for the Theory of Social Behavior* 92 (1979) 139–66.

Tillich, Paul. *The Courage to Be*. Glasgow: William Collins, 1977.

———. *A History of Christian Thought*. New York: Touchstone, 1967.

———. *The Shaking of the Foundations*. Harmondsworth, UK: Penguin, 1966.

———. *Systematic Theology I*. Chicago: University of Chicago Press, 1951.

———. *Systematic Theology II*. Chicago: University of Chicago Press, 1957.

Tracy, David. *Blessed Rage for Order: The New Pluralism in Theology*. New York: Seabury, 1975.

Wallace, James A. *Imaginal Preaching: An Archetypal Perspective.* Mahwah, NJ: Paulist, 1995.

White, Roger M. *Talking about God: The Concept of Analogy and the Problem of Religious Language.* Farnham, UK: Ashgate, 2010.

Williamson, Clark M. *Way of Blessing, Way of Life: A Christian Theology.* St. Louis: Chalice, 1999.

Wilson, Paul S. *A Concise History of Preaching.* Nashville: Abingdon, 1992.

———. *The Four Pages of the Sermon: A Guide to Biblical Preaching.* Nashville: Abingdon Press, 1999.

———. *Setting Words on Fire: Putting God at the Center of the Sermon.* Nashville: Abingdon, 2008.

Wimberley, Edward. *Moving from Shame to Self-Worth: Preaching and Pastoral Care* Nashville: Abingdon, 1999.

Wolff, Hans H. *Obadiah and Jonah: A Commentary.* Translated by Margaret Kohl. Minneapolis: Augsburg, 1986.

Wurmser, Leon. "Shame: The Veiled Companion." In *The Many Faces of Shame*, edited by Daniel Nathanson, 64–92. New York: Guilford, 1987.

Zimany, Roland D. *Vehicle for God: The Metaphorical Theology of Eberhard Jüngel.* Macon, GA: Mercer University Press, 1994.

Subject Index

absolute dependence, feeling of,
  63–67
analogia entis, ix, 37, 73, 92, 94,
  111–13, 115–19
analogia fidei, ix, 22, 37, 92–93, 109,
  116–19
analogy, ix, xii, 1, 9, 32, 36–38, 90–93,
  95–97, 100, 103–9, 111–23, 133
analogy of advent, 104, 109, 111, 116
Aquinas's analogical theology, 103–4,
  106–9, 114–15

correlational method
  and "answering theology," 63, 68,
    71, 79–80
  and existentialist philosophy,
    68–75, 76–79
  and modern theology, 35–36
  and pitfalls, 31, 36, 58, 61–62, 69,
    86–87, 89
  and preaching, viii–xi, 14, 29,
    40–41, 58–61, 82–89
  and psychotherapy, 75–76
  and Rahner, 76–78, 86
  and Schleiermacher, 63–68, 85
  and Tillich, 68–76, 85
  Tracy's approach, 82
  as two-way street, 79–84

demythologization, 45–47
diagnosis in preaching, 15–17, 31
divine *therapeia*
  definition of, viii, 35
  and analogues, ix, xii, 1, 9, 32, 36,
    90–93, 116–17, 119, 133

and metaphors, xii, 36–37, 90–91,
  119–23, 133

existentialist philosophy, 68–75,
  76–79

faith as courage, 76–78
Fosdick's project method, 2, 4, 9, 11,
  13–14

God
  in Aquinas's thought, 103–4, 106–9,
    114–15
  in Barth's thought, 42–43, 110–18
  incomprehensibility of, 98–106
  Kantian approach, 104–5
  and metaphors, 91–97
  in Maximus the Confessor's
    thought, 101–2
  in Przywara's thought, 113–15
  in Pseudo-Dionysius's thought,
    98–101
  as subject of sermon, vii–viii, x–xi,
    7–10, 34–35, 39–45, 48, 51,
    54–55, 57–61, 85, 119–20,
    122, 133–34

imaginal preaching, 26–29

Jonah
  and divine confrontation, 134–40
  and theories of the self, 139–40

Kantian philosophy of religion, 104–5

Author Index

23909900R00092

Printed in Great Britain
by Amazon